ONE AND HOLY

ONE AND HOLY
The Church in Latin Patristic Thought

ROBERT F. EVANS

Published for the Church Historical Society

LONDON

S·P·C·K

1972

No. 92 in the
Church Historical Series

First published in 1972
by S.P.C.K.
Holy Trinity Church
Marylebone Road
London NW1 4DU

Printed in Great Britain by
The Camelot Press Ltd, London and Southampton

SBN 281 02725 0

To
Henry Chadwick, D.D.
Dean of Christ Church
in gratitude

CONTENTS

INTRODUCTION

Those who occupy themselves with the history of Christian thought in the patristic period have often had cause to notice that between the Latin and Greek fathers of the Church there appears an unmistakable difference in the form or shape of their thought. The prevailing preoccupation of the Greek fathers is to bring the articles of Christian faith into adjustment with currently prominent themes and problems of Greek philosophy such as the concepts of God, providence, and the soul, and the relation between God and the cosmos. Concentration upon these matters led directly to the two great controversies of the fourth and fifth centuries, which were largely matters of Eastern dispute: the Trinitarian, or Arian, controversy, and the Christological controversy. While the Western Church did not remain passive regarding the issues in these controversies once they had arisen, Latin theology none the less shows a tendency to be concerned with a different set of problems which can best be identified as having to do with the form and character of the Christian society, or, to speak more briefly, with the doctrine of the Church

These, of course, are generalizations; one knows that the Latin fathers Augustine and Tertullian both wrote widely read and influential treatises on the problem of the Trinity. But as generalizations on the character and direction of Greek and Latin theology they seem to me sound. As symptomatic of the difference suggested here we may point to the two most imposing fathers of the ancient Eastern and Western Churches respectively: Origen and Augustine. If one were to select one writing from the corpus of each as more than any other work gathering up the various strands of its author's thought and presenting it in comprehensive fashion, one would doubtless choose Origen's *de Principiis* and Augustine's *City of*

God, and one could do this without falling into the anachronistic trap of calling either of these a work of 'systematic theology'.

The two works in fact bear interesting similarities to one another. They both sketch an entire cosmic history which begins with the creation of spiritual beings prior to any physical universe, continues through the long drama of God's relation to rational creatures once they have been set within the created cosmos, and ends in the final blessedness of the heavenly kingdom to come. Along the way they both treat the origin and nature of evil, the nature of the soul, and the problem of human freedom in relation to divine providence, to select only a few prominent and common themes. Among all the Latin fathers Augustine stands alone in the degree to which his thought is heavily informed by Greek philosophical currents.

Yet for all this the contrast between the two works is all the more striking. The Western and Latin stamp of Augustine's *magnum opus* is evident in its title and in the meaning of the title displayed in the contents of the work. For the city of God is none other than the Church, the Church which has its first beginning in the unfallen angels before man is ever created and which remains eternal in the heavens, the Church whose earthly members are now in the time of their pilgrimage towards their heavenly destiny, the Church which shall one day reign complete and triumphant in undistracted and eternal blessedness.

There is a second and closely related aspect in which the *City of God* both stands contrasted to Origen's *de Principiis* and exemplifies the Latin tradition. This is a particular form of duality which is not simply that between good and evil, spirit and flesh, temporal and eternal, or good and bad exercise of human freedom. These forms of duality play important roles in Augustine's thought, but they are accompanied and associated with another: over against the city of God is the city of man, the *civitas terrena*. Contrasted to the *civitas* willed and created by God is that created by man, whose concrete forms are the political units into which human society has organized itself ever since Cain built the first city in the book of Genesis. The stark and pervasive contrast between 'city of God' and 'city of man' in Augustine's work is in fact his own way of formulating the tension between Church and civil society which is a recurring preoccupation of Latin Christendom.

It is important to emphasize the word *Christendom* in the foregoing sentence, as we have here to do not with some perhaps favourite pastime of Christian intellectuals nor even only with a central theological topos. The papacy itself is to be seen as the most imposing institutional expression of the problem, and the papal theory of Leo the Great in the fifth century as one of its most enduring intellectual monuments.

It is my intention in the five chapters which follow to throw into relief the main contours of a tradition of thought by examining that tradition at certain of its major and critical phases. Our concern is with a way of conceiving the nature of the Christian Church and of its relation to the 'city of man' which originated at the beginning of Latin theology and which through many permutations and paradoxical turnings maintained its identity so as powerfully to condition the minds of Western Christian theologians in modern times whenever they have turned their attention to the problem of the Church. It would be instructive to pursue these inquiries through the medieval, reformation, and modern periods, but our business here is with a period which extends from the beginning of the third century to the beginning of the seventh. These limits are not simply arbitrary, since Tertullian in the third century set Western thought about the Church on that way which, at the turn of the seventh century, the great Roman Pope Gregory both brought to one of its major resting places and opened out to the medieval world beyond. To say as much as we have said here is to postulate a basic unity of thought among the five writers to be examined, and the basis for such a postulate will, I hope, become clear in the pages to follow. This unity, however, is much more a unity in conceiving the constituents of the problem than it is a unity of teaching. Of disagreement in precise doctrine of the Church among our authors there is no end, as we shall see.

1

TERTULLIAN:
THE UNITY OF THE SPIRIT AND
THE ONE FAITH

Tertullian of Carthage is the first Christian to have left for posterity a corpus of theological writings whose language is Latin. He was a layman, a moral rigorist, a rhetorician, a lawyer, and an African. He never, as far as we know, gave the sort of sustained and precise attention to thought about the Church that would have issued in a treatise 'On the Church'. Yet 'in his writings the problem of the Church is well nigh everywhere present. As he writes against Gnostic and Marcionite heresy the questions of the identity or 'unity' of the Church and of the criteria of the Church's authentic teaching come immediately to the fore. As he writes his moral treatises two problems are at once present: the relation of moral 'purity' to that holiness which he sees as one of the marks of the Church, and the relation of the society of Christians to the wider society in which they are set. As he writes his apologetic treatises in defence of the Christians before the non-Christian public, the second of the latter two problems is present in a special form: how is the 'shape' of the Christian community to be presented in such a way as to set that community in the most favourable light possible and yet in such a way as not to deny its special character?

Through all of these ways in which the problem of the Church presents itself to Tertullian there permeates a further issue which can be seen as twofold, yet is at the bottom one: what are the consequences, for the Church as a historical community, of its being indwelt by the Spirit of God, and what must the posture of the Church be as it awaits the indubitable and imminent end of all things? The themes of the Spirit and of eschatology are themes of the most crucial urgency for Tertullian;

they are themes which are integrally bound to his moral rigorism and which finally moved him outside the Catholic Church to join himself to that rigorous and Spirit-conscious Christian sect, the Montanists.

Though Tertullian is the first Latin Christian writer, he does not offer our first literary evidence of Christianity in Africa. That evidence, apart from an early African Bible text, comes from an event which took place in the year 180, when Tertullian was a young man of about twenty, and before his own conversion to Christian faith. Twelve native African Christians, seven men and five women, were put to death in that year by order of the proconsul Saturninus, a man who Tertullian himself tells us was the first Roman official in Africa to 'use the sword' against the Christians.[1] The incident is of interest here both because it introduces the fact of martyrdom in Africa within Tertullian's own life-span and thus sets the stage for one of his own lasting concerns, and also because the words spoken by one of the martyrs before the proconsul offer brief but eloquent testimony of that way of conceiving the life of Christian commitment which was to find extended development in the writings of Tertullian. The spokesman of the twelve, soon to meet their death, rejoined to the proconsul in part as follows:

> I do not acknowledge the imperial realm of this world; rather I serve that God whom no man has seen nor can see with his eyes . . . I do acknowledge my Lord, the king of kings and the imperial ruler of all peoples.[2]

To speak in this way was to speak in a clearly revolutionary spirit, and Tertullian, too, was a revolutionary.

In this context, 'to be a revolutionary' has in itself no direct bearing upon the means to be employed in the attaining of desired goals, and certainly is not meant to suggest that Tertullian either directly or indirectly encouraged Christians to engage in violent tactics towards the overthrow of the Roman imperial government. That he did not. Rather, 'to be a revolutionary' here means to be committed to a way of life of which both the presuppositions and the practical working out are at radical variance from the norms and practices of an established and widely accepted pattern of life.

The Roman state gods are the protectors and guarantors of Roman peace and security—that is the official assumption common to emperors, lesser magistrates, legal theorists, and patriotic rhetoricians of the pagan society which forms Tertullian's environment. As founder of that new order which we call 'the Roman Empire', Augustus in the first century B.C. had seen his task as one of ensuring the permanent endurance of concord and peace after the acute disorder of the recent civil wars and after the recurring disaffection and upheaval which had marked the history of the Roman republic for over a century before. One of the bulwarks of this imperial policy was the thorough rehabilitation of the cults of the state gods. The endurance and well-being of the empire required the active benevolence of the gods; the 'Roman peace' was dependent upon the 'peace of the gods'. Religion—*religio*—was precisely the entire system of cultic obligations which bound the people of the empire to their gods and through which they ensured the gods' continuing good will. Laws governing religion, therefore, formed a compartment of civil law.

Two further prominent elements appear as integral parts of developing imperial ideology: the notion of the unending permanence of the Roman order—'eternal Rome'—a permanence predicated upon the diligence with which the requirements of 'religion' were henceforth to be discharged; and the idea, to which ancient and oriental theories of kingship richly contributed, that the emperor himself is a sacral, even quasi-divine, personage, that while he lives and rules here he is at least last among the gods and first among men, and that at his death he will take an undisputed place among the gods in heaven.

These ideas could be—and often were—fortified and bound together by a further motif among rhetoricians and philosophers who, for whatever reasons, found it to their purpose to offer rationalizations and eulogies of the imperial system. Zeus, or Jupiter, the king of the gods, presides over the cosmos and administers it with careful providence. The emperor is his earthly 'type', his earthly reflection, presiding over the whole expanse of 'the civilized world', the latter to be identified *tout court* with the Roman Empire. The highest of the gods bestows upon the emperor his throne and equips him both with that divine wisdom that is requisite for his awesome task as well as with those other, moral, virtues so prized by the Romans both in rulers and in ordinary men: piety towards the gods, faithfulness in human relationships, righteousness in giving to every man his due, and mercy (this last, so far as the emperor was concerned, having its chief application as mercy to the conquered). Thus the emperor is lifted to a plane where he is not only likened to a god, but is seen also as playing a strategic role in the governance of the cosmos: he is father of men, protector of men, and exemplar of human virtue. The motif of which we speak here, setting the emperor in a special relation to the highest of the gods, is found perhaps chiefly and originally in philosophical writers whose language was Greek, but we do well to mention it. It is reflected in Latin poet and historian alike in the two centuries preceding Tertullian, and Tertullian was no stranger to Greek philosophical writings.

To take note of the *mystique* attaching to the cult of the emperor is to prepare the way for our understanding of the virulence with which Tertullian both attacks the idolatry of Roman religion and defines the posture of the Christian Church over against the Roman state.[3] For him, in one of his prominent moods, idolatry and the institutions of the Roman empire are inseparable. It is, then, no surprise that we read the following words halfway through a work which Tertullian addressed to the general non-Christian public:

> It is therefore against these things that our business lies: against the institutions of our elders, against the authority of received authors, against the laws of the rulers of this world, against the arguments of the wise, against the past, against custom and 'necessary' submission, against oracular warnings, prodigies, and miracles—all of which things have fortified this fake religion of yours.[4]

Tertullian joins his polemic against the Roman state with a dual expectation: that martyrdom is what any Christian may expect at the state's hands, and that the present order of this world is soon to be overthrown by the final divine judgement. In this, of course, he is not without precedent in the Christian Church of the first two centuries, though his

B

polemic is shriller, more sustained, and less veiled than had usually been the case heretofore. We are only now, and gradually at that, coming to an awareness of the breadth and depth of political issues present in the pages of the New Testament. It cannot be our business here to canvass that large topic. We must be content to say that Tertullian gathers up and restates traditions which go right back into the New Testament writings and back also to Jewish sources which Christians had long since appropriated for their own purposes. The event of Jesus' own death made it not unnatural that his followers would take with special seriousness the gospel warning that they would 'stand before governors and kings' for his sake, not supposing that a servant is greater than his master and that they might escape persecution any more than he had. And as for the 'peace and security' slogans of the imperial apologists, the Apostle Paul warned, 'When people say, "There is peace and security", then sudden destruction will come upon them'. The eschatological hopes of the early Christians posed a direct challenge to all thought of 'eternal Rome': 'Here we have no lasting city, but we seek the city which is to come'; 'our homeland is in heaven'. The book of Revelation gathers many such themes together in its apocalyptic outlook, in its exaltation of martyrdom, in its designation of the altar of the emperor-cult at Pergamum as the throne of Satan, in its threatening predictions of the downfall of Rome which is Babylon, the mother of whores and of obscenities, and in its vision of the holy city Jerusalem descending from God out of heaven.[5]

Although the above remarks will not serve as a balanced presentation of the teaching of the New Testament as a whole regarding the secular powers, they will help to indicate that the simultaneous presence in Tertullian's writings of a vivid eschatological hope, the theme of martyrdom, and a critique of the state and its religion, is not without foundation in Christian tradition.

We have now to ask what bearing this complex of themes has upon Tertullian's idea of the Church. Its bearing is at least threefold, and we shall look at these interrelated matters one at a time. First, Tertullian conceives the Church in a thoroughly eschatological way as a company of sanctified men and women who, right now, are bound to lead the life of the kingdom of God to come. Although it is not quite true that he simply identifies the kingdom of God with the Church, he sees the Church so vividly as an outpost of that kingdom that it is clear the structure and quality of life proper to the kingdom are now in actual fact present in the Church; Christ is the 'imperial commander' to whom the Christian soldier *now* owes the complete obedience proper to his baptismal oath of allegiance; life in the Church is life which 'belongs to the kingdom'; baptism is the 'entrance to the heavenly kingdom'.[6]

It is this context where properly belongs Tertullian's language about the Church as 'mother', as Eve, and as 'bride of Christ'. In the fifteenth chapter of his homily on baptism he inserts an arresting gloss into a loose citation of Ephesians 4.4-6, a text whose ecclesiological bearing is evident in its words about the one body and the one Spirit, and whose eschatological bearing would have been abundantly apparent to him in the words, 'the one hope that belongs to your calling'. In citing the text he writes, 'one God, and one baptism, and *one Church in the heavens*',[7] the last phrase having no counterpart in the original. The gloss is nicely revealing. To speak of 'heaven', for him, is to speak at once of the kingdom soon to come with power from on high and of the present citizenship of Christians in the kingdom, and of the duty which this citizenship imposes on them. Thus when he turns to write an exposition of the Lord's Prayer, we find him, much perhaps to our initial surprise, starting to talk about the Church in his comments on the first clause, 'Our Father who art in heaven'.[8] In fact it is clear that he understands 'in heaven' to be a way of referring to 'our mother the Church'. His point is that in the opening clause of the prayer, God, viewed on the severe model of a Roman family father, is honoured as possessing his unique 'power' over his domestic establishment, and that the Church is here explicitly referred to as the 'family' 'embracing God and those who belong to him by legal right'.

The church that is our mother is, moreover, none other than Jerusalem built of God, soon to be 'let down from heaven', 'our mother from on high'.[9] As viewed through these images the Church is grounded in the atoning death of Jesus Christ. Tertullian gives expression to this theme in his allegorical exegesis of the creation of Eve from the side of Adam. Adam is a type of Christ, Adam's 'deep slumber' a type of the death of Christ, and Eve issuing from Adam's rib a type of the Church issuing from the wounded body of Jesus. Thus is Eve the Church, 'the true mother of the living'.[10]

The Church is thereby also the bride of Christ, and in respect of this teaching, too, the notes of urgency and of irresistible pull towards the future-and-present kingdom are clearly present. The time allotted to this world is finished, gathered up, wound up. Therefore the time is right now for Christians to conform themselves to that image of monogamous marriage presented both by Adam the type of Christ in his one marriage to Eve, and by the one Christ who took to himself the one Church for his spotless bride. For the Church to be the spotless bride of Christ means nothing else than that Christians order their lives by the purity that is inherent in the image of the bride itself and that is the only appropriate moral condition for those who know themselves to be standing at the end of the time of this world.[11]

In a treatise which Tertullian wrote on the way in which women of the Church should dress he gives striking expression to this eschatological sense of the Church in words which we cannot pass over without quoting.

> Today let God see you as he will see you then. . . . We are they, upon whom the ends of the ages have fallen. We are those whom God predestined before creation to exist in the extreme end of time. And so God disciplines us by our reproving and (so to speak) castrating the world. We are the spiritual and fleshly circumcision of all things, for both in the spirit and in the flesh we circumcise the things of this age.[12]

We are led naturally on to the second general conclusion which Tertullian draws from the complex of ideas stated earlier. There is a whole range of activities and occupations from which Christians must abstain if they indeed are the advance troops of the kingdom to come. Tertullian sees the whole of pagan society as so thoroughly pervaded by idolatrous religion that it appears absolutely necessary to withdraw Christians not only from positions of political responsibility but from some secular occupations as well. To use a term with connotations from a later age, the Church for this author is indeed a 'sect', contributing in no way to the 'establishment' and holding itself carefully aloof from it. We see this first of all in his attitude towards the holding of secular power. In his great work the *Apologeticum*, addressed to the governors of the Roman provinces, he can write as follows: 'Nothing is more foreign to us than affairs of state'; 'the Christian does not seek the office of aedile'.[13]

Interpreters of Tertullian who do not wish to see his attitude as quite so 'sectarian' may well point out that what the author is trying to accomplish in statements such as these is, in effect, to assure the rulers that in spite of the apparently revolutionary stance of the Christians, they, the rulers, have in fact nothing to fear from the Christians by way of insurrection or even of some other more orderly means of gaining political power. This indeed is Tertullian's chief aim. But the conclusion is not justified that the statements quoted above are mere empty rhetoric. At an earlier point in the same work the author, in a passing remark, uncovers one of the primary reasons why for him the holding of high office would have been impossible for a Christian, viz., that Caesars are 'necessary for the world', that very 'world' which in his view is soon to meet its end; and in the same sentence he lets it be unmistakably clear that Christians cannot be Caesars.[14]

But in another treatise, *de Idololatria*, addressed not to governors but to Christians, Tertullian reveals a second reason why Christians will not be found in public office, a reason which for him would be, more accurately, not a second one but the same one stated in a different way. It is in the highest degree unlikely, he argues, that a Christian could hold any variety of administrative office without being directly and personally involved in the ongoing practice of idolatrous religion; he would either be engaging in pagan sacrifices himself or lending the authority of his office to such sacrifices, he would be appointing persons to be caretakers of temples, he would be responsible for the collection of money for the support of temples, and the like.[15] Neither, incidentally, will a Christian be found in the office of magistrate, since this would place him in the position of passing final judgement on men's characters, of imprisoning and torturing them, and of sending some to their death. All of these actions Tertullian would understand to be clearly contrary to express commandments of Christ.

It is true that the treatise in question here somes from Tertullian's Montanist and more rigorous period. It would be gratuitous, though, and in fact wrong to assume that the man changed his mind on every subject of importance on becoming a Montanist, and there appears to be no evidence that he changed it in this regard. It is clear, however, that Tertullian neither in his Catholic nor in his Montanist period spoke for all the Christians of Africa; indeed his remarks above are introduced by the comment that there had recently arisen a dispute as to whether a 'servant of God' could assume public office.

Public administrative office is not the only sort of occupation closed to Christians on the ground of complicity in idolatrous religion. We must remember that idolatry in Tertullian's mind is the supreme 'impeachment' which God the judge has to bring against the men of this world; it is the 'total cause' of their suffering the divine judgement.[16] Our author makes the relentless logic of the jurist serve both his clear awareness of the network of relations binding society together and his equally clear vision of the Church as a people set apart awaiting the end of the age. We should therefore not be surprised to find him proscribing all occupations which directly contribute to the practice of idolatry: the making of statuary for use in pagan worship; the purveying of sacrificial animals and the sale of incense for the same purpose; the art of the astrologer; schoolmastering, since schoolmasters have to catechize their pupils about the gods, and in any case it is expected of every schoolmaster that he will consecrate the first tuition-instalment from each pupil to Minerva; and professorships of literature, since teaching a subject matter is inseparable from commending it, and pagan literature is full of the gods from beginning to end.[17]

By a like logic Tertullian forbids a Christian to be a trainer of gladiators, on the ground that this is a business whose only end is the killing of men, of which a Christian can have no part.[18] Nor is military service open to him; even if one were successful in avoiding pagan sacrifice and the taking of men's lives, the baptismal oath of allegiance to God the Lord is absolutely

incompatible with the soldier's oath of allegiance to Caesar
the Lord.[19] If a Christian marries a non-Christian he has committed the equivalent of adultery.[20] One may not sign one's name
to a written financial contract containing an oath in the name of
a heathen god.[21] And one may certainly not pass one's leisure
hours in attendance at the public games in the circus, at the
dramatic productions in the theatre, or at the gladiatorial
combats in the amphitheatre. All these forms of amusement,
as shown in their historical origins, in the names of the gods
under whose auspices and for whose honour they are conducted,
and in their solemn pomp and regalia, are shot through and
through with the spirit and substance of idolatrous religion.[22]
In this context, writing in his pre-Montanist days, Tertullian
gives sharp utterance to the spirit of Christian separatism:

> O if only we were not waiting around in the same world
> with these people! But none the less we are separated from
> them in worldly things, for the world is God's but the goings
> on of this world are the devil's.[23]

There are two comments which must immediately be made
somewhat by way of footnoting the material just presented.
For one, Tertullian is all too well aware that he is having to
fight to establish and commend his position. There are church
people who take the line that to go to the shows is only to
provide oneself with innocent amusement at no cost to the inner
religion of mind and conscience.[24] Even Tertullian can scarcely
find language ('O hands to be amputated') to register his sense
of scandal that men who make idol-statues have even been
received into the ordained ministry.[25] If men protest that in
giving up the occupations which he proscribes they will have
no means of livelihood, he refers them to the Lord's parable
of the prudent builder who before erecting a tower sits down
to count the cost, and reminds them that it is laid on the Lord's
disciples to take up the cross and follow him.[26] If they complain
that, in order fully to live by the kind of radical obedience
which he is recommending, they will have to go out of the world,
the stinging rejoinder is returned: 'As if it were not worth
just as much to go out of the world than to stay in it as an
idolator.'[27] The Christian man is free, yes, free to devote
himself entirely to the avoidance of idolatry. Christians are

foreigners to this world, citizens of the Jerusalem that is to come. The Church is the ark of Noah, navigating cautiously amid the reefs and shallows of idolatry and, though there were ravens, kites, dogs, and serpents in that ark, no animal was there in which could be discovered the type of an idolator.[28]

And second, Tertullian in spite of all this does not wear blinkers that completely obstruct his vision; he is not unable to make distinctions concerning the life of that society whose general character he seems so to abhor. Writers on this author are careless who allow themselves to allege, say, that he advocates withdrawal from most forms of gainful employment. Rather he may be seen more accurately as foreshadowing the idea of a Christian ghetto. Artisans are to continue to ply their trade so long as they do not contribute directly to the institutions of idolatrous religion: the plasterer will mend roofs, lay on stuccoes, and decorate the walls of houses with ornamental reliefs, taking care not to delineate likenesses of gods; incense is of use to men generally for medicinal purposes, and to Christians it is of use for funereal purposes; and if a woodworker can carve a statue of Mars, he certainly knows how to put together a chest. True it is that you get more money for building temples and carving idols, but the demand for these jobs is only occasional at best. Let Christians be satisfied with less lucrative but more regular requirements—making shoes, building houses, tenements, baths, even official residences—knowing that 'smaller wages are compensated by more frequent earning'.[29]

We find Tertullian engaged in some rather nice causuistry when he feels himself being backed into an uncomfortable corner. The festivities of private rather than public life are more susceptible of being detached, at least in thought, from their common superstitious accoutrements. Marriage, for example, is an honourable estate and owes nothing to any idol. Therefore, if a wedding invitation does not specifically state that I am being invited to assist at a sacrifice, I will go, and will even consent to looking on while a sacrifice is being performed, knowing that by being there I am doing service to my friend who is a man, not to an idol.[30]

Tertullian is aware, of course, that he owes much too much himself to the learning and literature of this world to make the case at all plausible that a Christian should not enter upon that education in rhetoric and letters from which his own thought and writing so richly profited. He feels keenly the bite of a question whose assumptions would seem so self-evident to educated men of his age and which he formulates with a Christian twist as follows: 'how' (if one were not to study pagan literature) 'could anyone be trained up to ordinary human prudence *in the time that is left* or to any capacity for thought or action, since a literary education is the means of training for all life? *How do we repudiate secular studies, without which sacred studies cannot be pursued?*'[31] The answer is that a pupil who is a believer, once he can recognize idolatry as such, exercises his own discretion in selecting and accepting what is useful to him in the set curriculum; before God the judge he can always plead the legal excuse of *necessity*, i.e. can claim that the standard curriculum is the only path open to him for learning; and in contrast to the teacher, the pupil can more easily be absent from the pagan solemnities incidental to the running of a school. To teach the traditional literary curriculum is one thing and is forbidden; to be a pupil in this curriculum is another and is permitted.[32]

We come now to the third general conclusion which we find Tertullian applying to the character of life in the Church. In being the advance troops of the kingdom of heaven, the Church does not conduct its warfare after the manner of the armies of this world. Strict obedience to their commander Christ requires not only that Christians abstain from responding in kind to attacks upon their persons and property but that they positively respond by living now in that peace and freedom from fear of this world and its threats which are the marks of their kingdom. This theme is expressed at the more intellectual and reflective level by the commendation of a virtue which Tertullian calls 'patience'. In taking up this subject in a short and winning tract, he offers a Christian reworking of one of the venerable themes of Stoic philosophy. The old theme was well suited to his purpose. The Stoic texts variously describe patience as the knowledge of the things to be endured and of the things not to be endured, that virtue which above all has given the Stoics the reputation of being themselves hard to bear, the voluntary and long lasting endurance of things unpleasant and difficult. For our Christian moralist patience could well be described as that virtue which above all would make the Christians to their pagan contemporaries a subject of bafflement, a source of uneasiness, and a target of hostility, so separatist and apparently revolutionary did they appear and yet so apparently passive and ready to go to their death.[33]

In the pages of his tract Tertullian allows us to see Christians bereaved by the martyrdom of their loved ones, robbed of their property, subject to verbal abuse and to physical violence. They are to endure all of this, first because patience belongs to the nature of God and is supremely exemplified in the example of Jesus Christ who, on the night before going to his death, would not allow even one disciple to draw his sword.[34] But second they are to endure it because of their secure expectation of the coming of 'that day'. Tertullian's treatment of the theme is so eschatologically conditioned that it seems wholly natural to him to define impatience as the mother of all sins. Sin from this perspective either means the impulsive rushing forward to grasp some good thing or it means the inability or unwillingness to persevere in the good through hardship. Tertullian's kind of Christian will be able to avoid both kinds of sin through the sure hope that he possesses as he looks forward to 'that day'.[35]

But at the more concrete and practically more momentous level the attitude which we are describing issues in the commendation of martyrdom. That this matter was of no little moment to Tertullian can be seen from the fact that he devoted no less than three writings to it and was probably also the final editor and part-author of the *Passio SS. Perpetuæ et Felicitatis*, which informs us of the martyrdoms of five Christians at Carthage in March of the year 202. Of relevance to us here are a few points amid much that could be said and that he did say. Martyrdom is an unconditional obligation binding upon all Christians, if that is the fate which is consequent upon confessing the name of Christ under interrogation and if there is no other way to avoid an act of idolatrous worship. Though in his pre-Montanist days he countenanced flight in time of persecution so as to avoid direct confrontation, and later reversed this position, there was never any question in his mind as to what must be done if one is brought before the authorities.[36]

Martyrdom is the clearest and most direct way to participate in the sufferings of Christ. Tertullian in large part shares that primitive Christian outlook to be gathered not only from Scripture but from numerous documentary sources scattered throughout the second and third centuries: the martyr, by his death for sheer love of Christ, finds the nearest possible imitation of the death of his Lord; the martyr is so closely identified with Christ that Christ himself is suffering in the death of the martyr; through this identification the martyr becomes peculiarly endowed with the Spirit of Christ, an endowment that is expressed in visionary experience and in the gift of prophecy. Tertullian, too, joins closely together the themes of martyrdom, of the union of the Christian with Christ, and of the special presence of the Spirit.[37] But then Tertullian also specifies martyrdom as the divinely appointed way by which Christians who have fallen into sin after their baptism may without question win the divine forgiveness. Baptism with blood is the second baptism.[38] The 'forgiveness of sins' for this writer is an idea, or a reality, which finds its proper context in the act of baptism, whether first or second. This is an important point whose further bearing will find mention below.

In an early work from his pre-Montanist days Tertullian gives us a surprisingly neutral report of a practice of which here he signals neither his clear approval nor disapproval. From what he tells us, we gather that it has been the practice of some Christians, who had been excluded from the Church's communion for committing sin after baptism, to go to the prisons to ask that the martyrs restore them back to the 'peace' of the Church.[39] We here come up against that rigorist conception of membership in the Church which we have already touched upon in part and will notice more fully below. Other martyrological sources from the second and third centuries encourage the conclusion that in some, probably widespread, circles of the Church, it belonged to the honour accorded to martyrs to suppose that, possessing the Spirit in such full measure as they did, they could on their own authority bestow an extraordinary forgiveness of sins, just as Tertullian reports. Here, he is writing to commend and encourage martyrs,* in

* In the third century the term 'martyr' covered not only those who had met their death but those who had been imprisoned as well.

prison awaiting probable death. It would not be surprising, therefore, if he were to avoid criticizing a practice which so much redounded to the honour of those whom he was writing to honour, even though he might have had some reservations. Whatever his real convictions might have been in those early days, we shall find him as a Montanist denouncing the practice which he here records. For our purposes it is enough now to take note of the practice and of the cluster of ideas attaching to it. We shall discover that the continuing practice on the one hand and the development of thought about the Church on the other come into sharp conflict both in the mind of Tertullian, and, in a different way, in the mind of Cyprian.

We have seen Tertullian pose a sharp antithesis between Caesar as lord and emperor, and Jesus Christ, or God, as lord and emperor. Centuries of hymnody, liturgical prayer, and theology have accustomed the ears of latter-day Christians to hear little more than a platitude when God is called a king. It requires an effort of imagination to hear the challenge, the rattling clang, of such language on the lips of a third-century African Christian. For Tertullian, it was a matter of reality much more than of metaphor. The substitution of Christ for Caesar is for him a signal touching off a whole series of further substitutions. Caesar's kingdom is set off against Christ's kingdom of which the Church is the present earthly colony. We are present at the beginning stages of the Western doctrine of the two societies, the two kingdoms.

It is a commonplace of today's theological discussion to say that religion has no language peculiarly its own and that religious discourse must perforce use metaphors and 'models', drawn from ordinary language. Is it right, therefore, to speak of Tertullian as engaging in the kind of radical 'substitution' of which we speak rather than of his use of particularly vivid 'models' in communicating his meaning? The point so stated only begs the question as to the 'meaning' which he wishes to communicate. Such 'meaning' can only be gathered from the way in which the 'models' are employed, from the 'tone' of his writings taken as a whole, and in particular from the posture of the Christian Church in relation to society which he delineates. Of particular importance here are that posture of separation which so clearly characterizes the Church in his writings and the plethora of 'models' which he introduces not by way of innocent metaphor but in order to drive home the point of that separatism. The Church as a society and as a kingdom has the elements of a structure modelled in very large part upon the Roman imperial society in which Tertullian lived, a structure which he intends to be understood as a substitute for the structure of that other society. The Church, it has been said, is a 'shadow empire'. This designation, though helpful and illuminating, should not be taken to mean that all of Tertullian's relevant language in this regard is specifically constitutional, imperial, or legal. He draws his terms from a wider range as well.

It would be tedious to catalogue here all of Tertullian's language which can be seen as contributing to the conception of the Church as a shadow-empire. Some illustrative samples will suffice. The distinction between the ordained ministry and the laity is a distinction between *ordo* and *plebs*, terms applied in secular language to the city councils and the common people respectively. The office of the ordained ministry is called by the constitutional term *honor*, designating the sublimity of high public office. The assembled ministry constitutes a *consensus*, a body having the right to 'sit together' for judicial purposes. The order of the ministry is sacerdotal; the Christian Church has its own sacrifice offered to God, that of its eucharistic meal. The bishop is the local church's 'chief priest', *summus sacerdos.*[40]

One of Tertullian's favourite ways of talking about life in the Church is by the use of military language. In itself this is of course nothing new. Scripture and previous Christian tradition offered ample precedent. Added to this were prominent non-Christian precedents: the Stoic philosophers, with their talk of life as a military campaign, and the Eastern mystery religions, now making great headway in the Latin world, with their talk, for example, of the sacred cohorts enrolled in the service of the goddess Isis. Important for our understanding of Tertullian's usage, however, is the cardinal assumption that Christians may *not* serve in the emperor's army. This latter army does not, therefore, serve simply as the source of a group of metaphors; it stands in sharp contrast to the Christian army.

Military language was well suited to Tertullian's view of the strenuousness and unconditional obligation of Christian life. Christians constitute the *militia Christi*; the soldiery of Christ. At their baptism they enter upon a *sacramentum*, a solemn oath of allegiance to their commander. The standard of this army is the cross, and Tertullian with mocking ridicule elaborates on the point that all the standards worshipped by the Roman soldiers in their camps have as their basic but hidden structure the form of a cross—a fine exemplification of his cry, 'Everything in the world is unreal, nothing true.'[41] The Christian army even has its own version of standing guard—the observance of *stationes*, special fasts; a man who has placed himself under this obligation, it is interesting to note, is encouraged by Tertullian none the less to come into the 'camp' where Christians are celebrating the Eucharist, to take into his hands some of the sacramental bread, but to reserve it to be eaten after his fast is over. The imprisonment of the martyrs is the pre-battle rigour necessary to any successful contest. The crown for which this soldiery grasps is that of the martyr, the Roman soldier's crown of laurel being entirely inappropriate to it.[42]

If a Christian is pressed by those in authority to take on the office of a magistrate of this world, let him know that he will have ample opportunity to be a judge over the men of this world in the kingdom to come, and let him here and now turn down the office, if necessary by martyrdom. If a Christian longs to join the joyous throngs at the public festivals, let him know that the Church has its own calendar of festivals. And as for the shows and spectacles, Tertullian paints a picture, wondrous in its grim detail, of that everlasting spectacle which Christians will enjoy from their vantage point in the new Jerusalem—of kings and governors, actors, wrestlers, and charioteers, all tortuously tossing in the fiery billows of hell.[43]

This is the proper context in which to point to the pervasive presence of legal conceptions in Tertullian's thought. He would have been baffled by the way in which Christians of later centuries have found so obvious an antithesis between a legal and an eschatological conception of the Church, between Law and Gospel. For him, as we have seen, to speak of the Church eschatologically is to speak of it as an eschatological community. The Church of the heavens is already present now and will endure in the fully realized kingdom of heaven. But an enduring community is a community with structure, a structure articulated by law. The gospel would do nothing for men if it did not encompass them with a concrete means of ordering their lives together, a means of defining their obligations one to another and to God. It is the business of law to do this. Within the society of the Western Roman empire, one of whose most impressive practical and intellectual achievements was the development of its law and of legal theory; it would seem to the jurist Tertullian that to present the gospel as law is to present it in the one way that will permit it to take hold of men's lives.

Such a conclusion would have seemed even more evident to Tertullian on the basis of his and the Church's protracted effort to uphold the authority of the Old Testament in the face of Marcionite rejection of it. It seems utterly natural to him, in reference to Christ's 'fulfilling of the law and prophets', to call Christ the 'filling up' (*supplementum*) of the law, to speak of his 'amplifying' the law, of the 'fulness of law' being present in him. The gospel is 'our own law'.

Law has a further kind of relevance in Tertullian's thought. It is in the conception of law that two lines of thought, sometimes seeming to be opposite in their direction, in fact have their meeting place. Is Tertullian the revolutionary and Christian separatist really at odds with the Tertullian who can seem on occasion to be so world-affirming and who believes that the soul of every man is 'by nature Christian'?[44] No, they are one. Tertullian has a firm hold upon the Christian doctrine of creation. His polemic is not against the world of God's creation but against the world as led captive by the demons. Nor is he opposed to human government as such but only to the idolatrous pretensions of the government under which he lives.[45] For him, the doctrine of creation would appear to mean, among other things, that he can draw liberally upon the Stoic doctrine of 'nature' and of 'natural law'. Though the souls of men are now by and large held captive by demonic powers, those souls have within them a 'silent deposit of inborn knowledge', a 'testimony' which largely remains buried in oblivion but which even in pagans can and does assert itself in 'eruptions' from below. Such eruptions come from that divinely given 'nature' in which man as such participates. Before the giving of the Mosaic law the ancient patriarchs lived by the unwritten law of nature.[46]

On such a basis Tertullian could feel free to draw upon the teachings of pagan philosophers as they suited him and appeared to be congruent with Christian teaching. But on the same ground he could and did draw generously upon Roman legal conceptions. To do so was really in accord with his polemical and separatist stance. The Roman jurists were continually invoking the Stoic doctrine of natural law as their theoretical basis. Tertullian intended to undercut that appeal in the sense that he wished to remove all possible support from the idolatrous institutions of Roman society, institutions whose array stretched all the way from the private life of the humblest pleb to the ideology supporting the emperor and the authority of the emperor's government. But the idea of natural law itself, as well as numerous principles derivable from it in the formation of Roman positive law, Tertullian welcomed as grist for his mill. We shall have occasion below to notice a few such principles of law as they appear in contexts relevant to our interests in this chapter. He on the one hand claimed the doctrine of natural law as an expression of the Christian doctrine of creation and on the other tacitly admitted that a rather large number of conceptions in Roman positive law were in fact in accord with this natural law and were usable in ordering the life of the Christian society.

It is pertinent here to call attention to another and related sense in which Tertullian's 'world denying' outlook needs to be clarified, and perhaps qualified. Particularly in his apologetic works he can write as if he does not really assume either that the Church and the empire need necessarily and permanently be at odds with one another or that the end of the world and the final judgement need necessarily and literally be at hand. Christians not only pray for the emperor but pray also for the continued endurance of the empire and for Roman interests in general; they pray 'for the delay of the end', not at all desirous of experiencing the final cataclysms and knowing that the end is put off precisely by the temporal blessing brought to the world by Roman government. Just let the emperor acknowledge that he is but a man.[47]

In line with such sentiments Tertullian can urge the governors that persecution of Christians is out of accord with accepted legal theory and practice, and can suggest also that a policy of toleration towards the Christians would find precedents in current Roman practice. These precedents, on examination, appear all the more plausibly to argue for toleration of the Christians in that Christian practice can be seen to commend itself as superior to that of groups now tolerated. The mystery cults are allowed their secret meetings where depravities are practised which are utterly unlike the elevated proceedings of the Christian mysteries. The little 'corporations' recognized by the law, which serve as burial clubs and as social and cultic centres for humble folk, are to be compared to the Church in a number of respects, except that the Church's treasury is not in fact a repository of required and minimum dues paid by each member, and its money is not used to finance the brotherhood's occasional orgies of eat and drink; contributions to church funds are entirely voluntary, are commensurate with the giver's means, and are used only for meeting the minimum needs of the poor.[48]

The line of thought here indicated is of interest in displaying the kind of analogies which occur to Tertullian as he tries to present the Church to a pagan public in terms which that public would readily understand. But it is of further interest in suggesting that Tertullian, in common with many other Christians who have held impending and vivid eschatological hopes, is ready to view the course of this world's history as not necessarily coming to an imminent close; he is willing at least to entertain the idea that the Church might have an unfolding future in a revised and more constructive relation to the world.

It was the co-presence of Tertullian's legal frame of mind with his understanding of the operation of the Spirit of God that led him to some of the issues for which he is often best remembered on matters concerning the Church. For him, drawing upon Stoic thought, 'spirit' is *the* designation *par excellence* of what God is; 'spirit' is the 'substance' of God. But 'spirit' is also the name of one of the three 'persons' of the deity, to use the term which he first applied to the members of the triad of Christian tradition.[49] 'Spirit', then, has this dual signification in his mind: 'spirit' is what God basically is and 'spirit' is the name of one of the divine persons. The history of

c

redemption recorded in the Scriptures and seen through the eyes of Christian tradition as appropriated by Tertullian, is a history of an unfolding 'dispensation' in which God, through centuries of preparation, schools his people for the coming of Jesus Christ, who after his victorious return to the Father, pours out his Spirit upon his people. This people is the Church, whose vocation is to lead the life of the Spirit here and now in a world that will soon pass away; the Church is the colony, the outpost, of the heavenly kingdom to come. To his understanding of this scheme of redemption Tertullian brought a legal frame of reference and a disposition of mind highly sympathetic to the moral rigorism which also formed a prominent aspect of Christian tradition. He brought also his inclination towards Stoic language about the Divine as 'spirit' permeating and animating the world. The final result of this confluence of elements in Tertullian's mind was a conception of the Church as a body of people enlivened totally by the Spirit of God, and enlivened in such a way that they could and should express their 'spiritual' way of life in ethical requirements which, in their rigour go beyond the precepts and the example of Jesus Christ himself. When he became disenchanted with the Catholic Church, he found a home in the Montanist sect, two of whose chief marks were moral rigorism and new out-pourings of the Spirit in gifts of prophecy and of vision.

From an empirical, institutional, and legal point of view the identity, or unity, of the Church universal for the Catholic Tertullian is constituted by the acknowledgement in all the local churches of the binding authority of the 'rule of faith', that summary exposition of the chief headings of revealed doctrine, variable in its precise wording but immutable in its dogmatic substance. In the fullest exposition which Tertullian gives of this rule, it includes belief in one God, the creator of the universe; in Jesus Christ his Word and Son, who was born, who preached, was crucified, was raised from the dead and taken again to the Father in the heavens; on the Holy Spirit; and in the coming judgement and resurrection of the flesh.[50] That this summary should be called a 'rule' (*regula*) is most probably due to the atmosphere of controversy with Gnostics, which would make it natural to point to a long standing summary of catechetical teaching as a 'standard', or 'rule'.

In Tertullian's usage 'rule of faith' is an equivalent for a number of other terms, all of which can denote the central doctrinal content of Christianity: 'law of faith', 'teaching', 'faith', and even (in one of its meanings) *'sacramentum'*, a Latin equivalent for the Greek *'mysterion'*, i.e. the sum total of the 'holy mystery' of Christianity expressed in doctrinal formulae.[51]

In a famous writing against the Gnostics, *de Praescriptione Haereticorum*, Tertullian makes important use of the rule of faith in a way particularly revealing for our purposes here. A close association emerges between, on the one hand, a *matter of faith* (surely if there ever was a dispute over the content of faith in early Christianity, it was that with the Gnostics) and the *ecclesiological issue* which Tertullian formulates in legal terms. We see the doctrine of the Church coming boldly forward to the centre of the stage in a way highly significant for the history of Latin Christian thought.

The bone of contention which Tertullian seizes upon in this writing is the Gnostics' appeal to the Christian Scriptures in support of their teaching. He states the issue between Catholics and Gnostics in terms of the legal right to possession: 'To whom belongs possession of the Scriptures?' To 'possess' the Scriptures, to employ them in the support of religious teaching, is the right of Christians. Are the Gnostics Christians? In the effort to return a negative answer to this question Tertullian makes use of further considerations from the law of property, in which the terms 'handing over', or 'delivery' (*traditio*), 'original owner' (*auctor*), and 'successor in possession' (*successor*), play important roles. Only those whom Christ appointed as Apostles may be accepted as the original preachers of his gospel, and it will be in those churches founded by Apostles where will be discovered the tradition of belief which they passed on.

Following directly from these points Tertullian invokes a line of argument which he took over from an illustrious predecessor in combating Gnostic heresy, Irenaeus of Lyons. The link between the Apostles as original *auctores* and the Church of later generations is provided in every church of apostolic foundation by a succession of monarchical bishops each one of whom serves in his time and place as the agent by whom the apostolic faith is 'handed over'. The historical continuity of this succession is attested by official rolls on which are recorded the names of the bishops as they have succeeded one another down to the present; each succession list begins with the name of the first bishop of that church and with the name also of the Apostle or disciple of an Apostle (*apostolicus*) who appointed the first bishop to his office and instructed him in the apostolic faith. Local churches founded since the close of the apostolic age properly enjoy the title 'apostolic' in that they have been planted by churches of apostolic foundation and in that they agree with those churches in adhering to the rule of faith. There is, therefore, a continuous stream of authoritative teaching, summarized in the rule of faith and preserved and handed on in the succession of bishops. To be in communion with the apostolic churches is to hold to the rule of faith, and the rule of faith in turn is the indisputable legacy of the Apostles, who owed their office to Christ. The conclusion follows directly: The continuous possession of the rule of faith by a regular process of *traditio* establishes those who hold to it as alone having claim to the name of Christian and as alone having rightful 'possession' of the Scriptures; a formal and devastating demurrer, or objection (*praescriptio*), has thus been entered into this projected legal action against the heretics, demonstrating that the Gnostics do not in the first instance have any right to those scriptures which they claim to possess.[52]

So wrote the still Catholic Tertullian. The precise argument concerning the succession of bishops is not, really, that every church claiming to be apostolic must be able to produce its own succession list going back to the Apostles. The argument from episcopal succession has rather to do directly with the churches of apostolic foundation and serves to buttress the apostolicity of the rule of faith, whose authority is now unanimously recognized in those very churches. The apostolicity of churches not able to claim apostolic foundation lies in their being 'offshoots' from churches of apostolic foundation and in their agreement with these churches in doctrine. It is not our business here to explore the various historical issues attendant upon the notion of a succession of monarchical bishops, but rather to set the problem of episcopacy in the context of Tertullian's developing thought. We shall find Cyprian later in the third century making some significant additions to this doctrine of the episcopate and thus developing it in one direction. Tertullian the Montanist developed it in another.

From one point of view, the Montanist Tertullian stayed close to the position stated above. He continued to regard the rule of faith as an indispensable mark of the Church. He argued that the Montanists' adherence to the rule proved that they were not heretics, since heresy, he thought, has to begin at the beginning, and overturns the foundation of the faith before it does anything else.[53] Tertullian can in fact go surprisingly far in asserting the oneness of the 'psychic'* church he has forsaken with the 'spiritual' church he has entered. We see this in his comments on certain Catholic churches of the East, churches which, in contrast to the lax African 'psychics', keep their virgins veiled as the Montanists think proper:

> One faith is common to them [the Easterners] and to us, one God, the same Christ, the same hope, the same baptismal sacraments; let me say it once and for all, we are one church.[54]

Only on the basis of this fundamental postulate of the continuing unity of Catholics and Montanists, can we understand Tertullian's enduring attention to problems within the Catholic churches as his own problems.

In the context of the remarks quoted above Tertullian makes an important point concerning vocabulary which we cannot fail to notice and which has relevance to his shifting notions of the apostolate, the episcopate, and the Spirit. To see how this is so, we must first fill in some details.

Tertullian's argument is that once the fixity of the rule of faith has been forever established, there needs to be a principle of movement, of development, of novelty at work in the Church, since the devil never ceases to find new ways of assaulting. This development will take place at the level of *disciplina*, 'discipline',[55] which Tertullian understands as encompassing ethics, penitential practice, and in fact everything that falls under the traditional heading of 'ecclesiology'; 'doctrine', on the other hand, *doctrina*, applies to the heads of theology encompassed by the rule of faith. This argument for development in 'discipline' he bolsters by two legal considerations.

---

* Tertullian as a Montanist took to calling Catholics by the epithet 'psychics' to designate their inferiority to the Montanist 'Spirituals'.

Custom, which often *is* a good guide to conduct and has the
force of law, should never on the other hand be opposed to
'reason', or 'truth', and whenever the two are found to be
opposed, it is always the latter which must carry the day.[56]
Second, there is the argument 'from the lesser to the greater',
which for Tertullian means that the Montanist Church (the
greater) must at the very least never be found lagging behind
the highest, most rigorous, ethical practices and conceptions
either of the heathen or of the Catholic 'psychics' (the less).[57]

Now to lead and to preside over this development in *disciplina*
is the function of the Spirit of God. As Tertullian writes in
the opening chapter of his work, *de Virginibus Velandis,*

> What, then, is the office of the Paraclete but this: the
> direction of discipline, the unveiling of the Scriptures, the
> re-forming of the intellect, and progress towards better things.
> Nothing is without stages of growth; all things await their
> proper time.

Thus Tertullian posits a growth in the requirements of
'righteousness' (for that is what interests him) in four acts
on the stage of human history: a rudimentary phase, at which
the 'natural' fear of God was operative; infancy, accomplished
through the Mosaic law and the prophets; youth, through the
gospel preached by Christ; and now maturity, to which the
Spirit is leading. Tertullian in this vein will tell us that we are
not in all cases allowed to look to the life of Jesus for authoritative example in conduct. Christian 'discipline' dates from the
renewal of the covenant, i.e. the Lord's passion; there were no
Christians before the return of Christ to heaven, no one holy
before the coming of the Spirit from heaven.[58] We observe
here one set of conclusions to which a concentration upon 'the
crucial events from Good Friday to Pentecost' can lead.

We are now in a position to see part of the relevance in the
point of vocabulary mentioned above. It has to do with the
word *antecessor*, a noun common in juristic texts meaning either
predecessor in office or teacher (of law), or both. From writings
in Tertullian's Catholic and Montanist periods, as well as from
other Catholic writers of the third century, it appears that
among Catholics the word both was applied to the apostles
as teachers of the bishops appointed by them, and was applied

also to the post-apostolic bishops as predecessors and trans-
mitters of tradition to their successors. In the same Montanist
work cited above, Tertullian, in his effort to uphold the authority of the Spirit in leading the Church to new and more
demanding levels of rigour, now asserts that the Spirit 'is the
only *antecessor* because he alone comes after Christ'. As opposed
to this, he lets us know that it is among the Catholics where
talk of multiple 'predecessors' still holds sway.[59]

What Tertullian has here done is to pound a heavy blow in
driving a wedge between a conception of the Church as Spirit-
filled, and Spirit-led, and a conception of the Church as an
institution with historical, empirical continuity and with its
regularized marks. These two conceptions had been present
concurrently in his pre-Montanist days without ever being
fully integrated. The Church possessed a Catholic teaching,
i.e. a teaching universally shared by the churches of apostolic
foundation and by their daughter churches, and this catholicity
of teaching was associated closely with the rule of faith and with
the episcopate.[60] But the Church as a whole was under the
tutelage of the Holy Spirit, and in this connection Tertullian
had introduced a term that was to have a long future (though
with other applications): the Holy Spirit is the *Vicar of Christ*,
Christ's deputy with plenipotentiary powers.[61] This formula
he now repeats and to it joins the assertion that the Spirit
is the 'only *antecessor*', the only teacher of the Christian law of
life.[62] To look at the matter from Tertullian's Montanist
point of view, we could say that the redemptive work of Christ
is brought to its fulfilment in the ongoing activity of the Spirit
moving the Christian community to a new and firmer grasp
of that ethical purity which is the will of God for his people;
as opposed to the unalterable rigidity of the rule of faith, which
it is the business of Catholic bishops to uphold, the 'discipline'
administered by the Spirit is, at least apparently, on the move;
the Spirit must be seen as having the freedom to draw the
Church towards divine requirements which historical honesty
must admit have not been universally and continuously
recognized in the Church in the way that the rule of faith has
been recognized. Though honesty must admit this much,
Tertullian at the same time insists that his present spiritual
teachings represent the real intention of the apostolic writers and

that his rigorism is suported by true exegesis of the Scriptures. In this sense he makes the claim: 'Of old we were being destined to this sanctity; the Paraclete is introducing nothing new.'[63] So far it is clear that Tertullian the Montanist assigns to the Spirit the crucial role of introducing into the Church apparent innovation in the sphere of discipline. This work of the Spirit proceeds quite independently of whatever the position of the Catholic episcopate might be. We must now notice that Tertullian comes to assign to the same Spirit an important role in the sphere of doctrine as well. He is far from agreeing with the proposition that bishops as such are organs of the Spirit, either in discipline or in doctrine.

In the opening chapter of his Montanist treatise on the Trinity, *adversus Praxean*, Tertullian waxes indignant both at the way in which obnoxious teaching concerning the godhead once made headway at Rome, and at the action of a bishop of Rome in refusing to recognize the Montanists. Though he does not follow his Roman contemporary Hippolytus in actually stating that the bishop of Rome has condoned the objectionable teaching (called 'Monarchianism', asserting the simple identity of Father with Son and Spirit), the most likely interpretation of Tertullian's veiled language is to see him aligning the Catholic rejection of Montanism alongside Catholic sympathy with erroneous teaching on the godhead. In any case he clearly asserts that a right understanding of the relations among the 'persons' of the godhead is due to the operation of the Spirit, and in fact links his own Trinitarian teaching directly to his Montanist allegiance.[64] This means in the end that the Spirit works not simply at the level of 'discipline' but at the level of 'doctrine' as well, bringing to pass the correct understanding of the relations among Father, Son, and Spirit, those three prominent headings of belief in the rule of faith. It is one of the nice ironies of Church history that Tertullian in a work put forward as expressing views of that Montanist sect outlawed by a bishop of Rome, formulated a vocabulary for the Western doctrine of the Trinity whose untiring champions were to be the Catholic bishops of Rome.

The authority of the Catholic episcopate in the realm of doctrine seems thus to have passed well into the background. In fact it has passed out of sight: this is the second aspect of the relevance of saying that the Spirit is the only *antecessor*. Though Tertullian does not say it in so many words, it would appear that with this formula he now has no need at all of the sort of historical arguments which as a Catholic he has used in establishing the authority of the rule of faith. The formula would give him ground for saying that that rule does not depend for its authority upon any succession of bishops but rather upon the direct working of the Spirit of God. Neither the rule of faith nor its proper interpretation in Trinitarian terms needs the witness of the Catholic episcopate.

We have seen the late Tertullian displeased with the Catholic 'psychics' over a specific doctrinal matter. It remains for us to find him similarly displeased over a specific disciplinary matter and at the same time to find him giving his most extreme expression to a 'spiritual' conception of the Church.

Tertullian from his Catholic days is a witness for a traditional rigorism, eschatological in its orientation, which tended to view the commission of sin after baptism as placing one outside the peace and communion of the Church.[65] Three sins in particular, sins 'against God', were regarded as having this effect: idolatry, murder, and adultery. For Christians guilty of one of these there was the sole expedient of 'second repentance', called also 'confession', and, by the Greek equivalent of the latter term, *exomologesis*. The sinner clothes himself in sackcloth and ashes, prostrates himself before both presbyters and people, and pleads for their intercession to God that he, the sinner, will be forgiven.[66] This procedure issues not in restoration to communion in the Church, but, as Tertullian reports, to virtual assurance that God will in the end forgive. In casting himself upon the prayers of the Church the sinner is in fact entreating Christ, since 'the Church is Christ', and God will not fail to hear his Son.[67] If serious sin is then committed again after 'second repentance' is undertaken, the sinner is lost without hope.[68] The possibility of a 'second repentance', and of its effect, seems to have spread out from Rome, beginning in the middle of the second century, through the circulation of an intriguing writing called *The Shepherd of Hermas*. Baptism is, of course, the first repentance, and Tertullian is only giving expression to a traditional view when he urges, on the ground of the grim seriousness of post-baptismal sin, that the receiving of baptism be postponed until one has settled into mature life, in particular that one not be baptized while still a young bachelor.[69]

We know from the writings of Hippolytus that Callistus, bishop of Rome, undertook an important revision in policy regarding serious sins and thus again put the church of that city in the vanguard of a progressive loosening of the ancient rigorism. Callistus announced that Christians guilty of sexual offence could be received back into full communion in the Church. It appears overwhelmingly probable that it was this action of the Roman bishop that called forth the Montanist Tertullian's angry treatise, *de Pudicitia*. Here he scornfully relates in his opening chapter that the '*pontifex maximus*', the 'bishop of bishops', has issued a 'peremptory edict' remitting the sins of adultery and fornication.[70]

As a Montanist Tertullian changed his views on 'second repentance' in two particulars: the kinds of serious sin to be regarded as unforgivable *by the Church* are increased in number, and he no longer regards second repentance as offering assurance of the divine forgiveness—at best it is a 'publication of disgrace'.[71] Whereas Tertullian would have us know that he has taken a large stride 'ahead' of the traditional discipline, the bishop has walked so far backward as to place himself outside the bounds of Christian discipline entirely.

The bishop of Rome appears to have based his action upon Jesus' words to Peter, 'On this rock I will build my Church . . . I will give you the keys of the kingdom of heaven, and whatever you bind on earth shall be bound in heaven, and whatever you loose on earth shall be loosed in heaven'.[72] The bearing of these words for Callistus seems not to have been in the direction of elevating the authority of the bishop of Rome in particular as the successor to Peter; that is a later development of which we shall take note in the next chapter. Rather the idea was that the authority given to Peter was an authority passed on to bishops as such.

To this Tertullian has two basic answers which are not entirely consistent with each other and whose mutual tension arises from the persistent lack of unity in Tertullian's outlook as between a really strict, consistent, rigorism and the special powers possessed by men of the Spirit. The first is to interpret the 'loosing' of sins in Jesus' words to Peter as applying properly to the forgiveness of sins in baptism. The second is to insist that the authority given to Peter in respect of post-baptismal sins has nothing to do with any supposed authority given to bishops. The business of bishops is to watch over and to serve the Church's discipline, not to preside over that discipline regally so as to destroy it. Peter, on the other hand, was the first man of all to be endued with the Spirit, an endowment amply evidenced by his recorded deeds in the Acts of the Apostles—his raising of the dead, his healing of the sick, his rigorous dealing with those who disobeyed the Church's discipline. The Apostles were men possessing a full endowment of the Spirit; they were not 'bishops'. It is to 'spiritual' men, if to any at all, that such power now belongs as that claimed by the miserable bishop.[73] Tertullian in this line of argument is willing to agree that the Church has power to forgive post-baptismal sins. This Church, however, is not a 'collectivity of bishops' but is simply the company of 'spiritual' men. Whereas Tertullian in arguing for the efficacy of second repentance had written, 'the Church is Christ', now he wishes to fix the eschatological purity of the Church in the most unmistakable way possible and does this by saying, 'The Church itself, both in its present identity and in its origin, is the Spirit himself'.[74]

Tertullian had once commented that the soul given to man in creation is not properly to be called 'spirit', because though the soul can sin, Spirit cannot.[75] It is clear that the Church of the redeemed, here identified with the Spirit, is a Church from which sin in any important sense is absent. But there is a second final conclusion to be drawn about the Church as identified with the Spirit. The motto 'No bishop, no Church' is at the farthest point removed from Tertullian's late thought. It would still be true to say that if there *had not been* bishops united in the role of faith there would now be no historical and empirical guarantee of an authentic Church. Tertullian, however, is now little interested in *this* kind of empirical consideration. Any two or three persons whom the Spirit gathers and who 'conspire' together into the faith of Father, Son, and Spirit, are themselves a Church.[76] But, to continue Tertullian's own sentence, his present formulation goes even further: 'The Church itself, both in its present identity and in its origin, is the Spirit himself, in which Spirit consists the

trinity of the one divinity, Father, Son, and Holy Spirit.'[77]
Which is to say, if we may dare to paraphrase, that just as the
term 'spirit' specifies the identity of the whole triune deity,
so in a closely analogous sense does the Spirit define the identity
of the Church. The Church is the irruption of the divine life
into the world; it is the place where take place those activities
of which God in a peculiar sense is the agent: the raising of the
dead, the healing of the sick, prophesying, and life in accord
with the most stringent standards of purity. It is only by people
possessing these gifts, if by anyone at all, that serious sin
can be forgiven, because the forgiving of such sin is the preroga-
tive of God.

This means that Tertullian is in effect adding (substituting?)
one kind of empirical criterion to another in answer to the
question, 'Where is the Church?' In the work on prescription
of heretics such criteria included the rule of faith, a succession
of bishops traced back to the Apostles in the case of churches
of apostolic foundation, and, in the case of later churches, the
fact of having been planted by churches of apostolic foundation.
Now the important criteria are the evidences of the Spirit, and
in the very latest of Tertullian's Montanist writings, these
criteria seem to have carried all before them, leaving the
others out of view.

The late Tertullian was and was not willing to agree to the
proposition that 'spiritual' men might forgive the post-baptismal
sins of others. He was afraid of the idea, lest it encourage men
to keep on sinning. And in particular did he announce at the
close of de Pudicitia that he was opposed to the martyrs' bestowing forgiveness on adulterers and fornicators. In order to make
his position plausible he adopted the line of argument, embar-
rassing for a Montanist, that the martyrs after all are only men,
who dare not take it on themselves to forgive sins reserved
for the judgement of God. If one wishes to justify the practice
of seeking forgiveness from martyrs by the traditional saying,
'Christ is in the martyr', the cynical rejoinder is returned that
the martyrs should prove Christ is in them by their power of
telling the secrets of the hearts of those whom they would
forgive. And Tertullian cannot escape the following legal
consideration: forgiveness of the adulterer will bring in its wake
forgiveness of the idolater as well, since crimes committed

involuntarily, in this case under the duress of persecution, are much less serious before the law than crimes committed voluntarily, and adultery is nothing if not committed voluntarily.[78] We have here an omen of the troublesome issue that was to arise early in the episcopate of Cyprian, bishop of Carthage.

The dual emphases of law and of Spirit have reached a very particular sort of synthesis in Tertullian's late thought on the Christian life. The function of the Spirit, apart from manifestations such as ecstatic prophesying and healing works, is to lead Christians into conformity to more and more exacting requirements of divine law and thus to throw into ever sharper relief the peculiar character of Christian life in anticipation of the coming life in the fulness of the Kingdom when the conditions and limitations of life here will be no more. Where the Spirit is, there is the Church. Where the Spirit is, there is the rule of faith, and there is obedience to the law of the Spirit in fastings, in the keeping of stations, in modest dress, in the strictest practice of monogamy, in careful abstention from everything idolatrous, in refusal to flee in time of persecution, and in holding to the conviction that there is no peace in the Church for those committing serious sin after baptism.

In Tertullian Law and Spirit are together seen as supporting and requiring the strict eschatological purity of all persons in the Church. Where there is not this purity, there is not the Church. The holding together of Law, Spirit, and purity in this way means for Tertullian that the purity of the Church is the criterion for discovering its unity in the Spirit and is in fact the criterion for establishing the boundaries of the Church. In his Montanist days he does want to argue that the Church of the 'spirituals' and the Church of the 'psychics' are really one Church on the basis of their common possession of the same rule of faith, the same eschatological hope, and the same sacrament of baptism, and such an argument gives us ground for not being entirely surprised when we do in fact find him arguing with Catholics as brothers in faith. But the argument really stands as an isolated surd in the midst of his final complex of conceptions. Though the Spirit may blow over the psychics, they do not breathe the Spirit. The Church is found wherever two or three breathe the Spirit, and the Spirit blows where it wills.

2

CYPRIAN:
THE EPISCOPAL BOND OF PEACE

Tertullian had written at a period when local and sporadic persecution of Christians was always a threatening possibility, and we know from his writings that such persecution occurred in Africa during his lifetime. None the less this persecution was in fact local and sporadic. If one takes the trouble to read between the lines particularly of Tertullian's apologetic writings, one can draw the impression, confirmed by Christian and pagan writers elsewhere, that the closing decades of the second century and the early decades of the third were on the whole a time when the fortunes of the Christian Church did not look entirely bleak, and a time moreover when the membership of the Church was noticeably on the increase. The reader of Tertullian may even infer indirectly, as we have seen, that that author is willing to consider at least the theoretical possibility of an armistice between Church and empire, on the unlikely supposition, of course, that the empire renounce all expectations and requirements that Christians participate in idolatrous religion. Tertullian, moreover, is a witness for a time when the administrative machinery of the empire as a whole had not yet been harnessed for a general and unified attack on the Church.

By the end of the year 250 the situation had changed. The middle decades of the third century saw the empire in acute distress in more than one way. Masses of 'barbarians' were pressing and overrunning the frontiers in the West, North, and East, the imperial armies meeting a discouraging number of defeats. Rebellion in the army caught up generals and troops alike and led to the demise of one emperor after another. In both East and West it was not unknown for whole provinces to establish and for years maintain a political independence of the empire. Naval command of the Mediterranean had strenuously to be fought for, and not always successfully. Heavy taxation was required for the military necessities, for various financial deals with enemy leaders, and for the celebration of Rome's millennium in 248. Inflation of the currency reached staggering proportions. And to all of this was added the ravage of a plague which seems to have claimed tens of thousands of lives.

In the middle of this picture the emperor Philip the Arabian in 248 gave to the military leader Decius command of the armies facing the Goths, who had suceeded in crossing the Danube. Decius' victory there prompted the troops to proclaim him emperor, a position which he was able to make secure for himself once he had defeated Philip's force at Verona. Thus did the new emperor in 249 undertake to push through a policy of restoration of the empire's integrity. The policy extended from an attempt to improve the discipline of the army among the border troops, through new tactics to keep at bay the barbarians on the northern and western frontiers, to a more general encouragement of the return to traditional Roman virtues and customs. In accord with the axiom that the peace of the empire depends upon the 'peace of the gods' Decius sought to enlist the efforts of Romans everywhere to secure that peace. He was, of course, well aware of the problem posed by the Christians. Early after returning to Rome from his victory at Verona he issued an order whose precise contents we do not know but which led to the arrest of bishops in a number of widely scattered cities.

But then in the year 250 came an edict that all citizens must perform a public act of sacrifice to the gods of the empire or go to their death. It is not necessary to suppose that this edict was directed specifically and primarily against the Christian Church; as observed above, Decius had in mind a positive policy of uniting the empire behind him in his efforts at restoration. The edict did fall heavily, of course, on the Christians.

Our intent above has been to sketch a minimal background against which to place the ecclesiological thought of Cyprian, who became bishop of Carthage only months before Decius' edict ordering a general sacrifice. Since Cyprian's developing thought is so intimately linked to the events of his episcopate, reference to some of those events will be unavoidable in what follows. It will not be our business, however, to follow through those events in detail, nor to defend by argument implied solutions to one or two difficult chronological problems relative to the historical placing of Cyprian's writings.

The general political and social malaise, coupled with the sudden darkening of the political situation relative to the Church, goes some way in offering explanation as to why Cyprian's writings do not deal more at length and more explicitly with the confrontation between Church and empire. It appears that Cyprian was an avid reader of Tertullian. Most of his non-epistolary writings deal with themes and problems in the writings of Tertullian and in their content betray dependence on that author. He had received the education in letters and rhetoric appropriate to the son of a rich and cultivated pagan family and was converted to Christianity as a mature man. His thought displays an eschatological orientation not unlike that of Tertullian, though not so vividly articulated. But once Cyprian had set aside his very early and short tract, *Quod Idola Dii non sint*, he only once again turned his pen to a clearly 'apologetic' writing. This is his address to one Demetrian in answer to charges that the recent calamities of famine, drought, war, and plague are attributable to the Christians. The work is both very short and restricted in scope in comparison with the extended apologetic of Tertullian. Cyprian in fact in this work and elsewhere writes as a man utterly convinced that the day of the Lord is at hand and convinced of this with such serenity that extended persual of the old apologetic themes is simply no longer to the point. In fact Cyprian could be said to be writing *apologetic* only in the sense of claiming the present and imminent vindication of Christian faith; the only thing to do is to assert the facts as Cyprian sees them and to invite Demetrian to repent and believe before it is too late. The failure of the crops, the absence of winter rains and of summer sun, the murderous plague, the raging of repeated wars, all offer ample testimony that the world is running down and will soon meet its final end. Christians have long known that 'in the last times evils would be multiplied and misfortunes varied'. These things are just as natural as the coming on of old age in a man, and no one thinks

of blaming Christians for the latter phenomenon.[1] These
disasters, moreover, are simply the concomitants of widespread social evils: corruption in the courts and the buying
off of judges, avarice in the market-place and in public life, the
wholesale and shameless seizure of the property of the dying.
And to all of this are added the abasement of the public in
degrading worship of crocodiles, snakes, apes, and stones,
and the persecution of the innocent Christians.[2] Physical decay,
moral evil, idolatrous religion, and the oppression of God's
own people are simply four indicators pointing in one direction:
the great and terrible day of the Lord when an avenging God
will take to himself those who have been signed with the blood
of Christ and will condemn the pagans to a gehenna whose
fire goes not out. So Cyprian to the proconsul Demetrian.

To fellow Christians Cyprian wrote in corresponding fashion
and with much repetition of motifs that in the previous chapter
we have already noticed in Tertullian. The longest section of his
de Exhortatione Martyrii is devoted to developing the theme that
in persecution nothing unexpected is coming upon the Christians, since Scripture has plainly predicted that the world
will hold them in abhorrence. The scriptural passage of which
he here makes most is the account in 2 Maccabees 7 of the
execution by Antiochus IV of seven Jewish brothers and their
mother in the early second century B.C., a piece of hagiography
long treasured by both Jews and Christians and a signal of
the Jewish origins of early Christian martyrology; the seven
brothers stand for the seven churches of the Book of Revelation.[3]
Christians are to pray earnestly that the martyr's crown may
be theirs; by it those who have been servants of God are made
his 'friends'. Martyrdom is also a 'second baptism'. But Cyprian
in contrast to Tertullian does not speak of this 'second baptism'
as a divinely appointed means by which the Christian may be
absolved of his own post-baptismal sins. A vestigial remain
of that teaching is found in the assertion that this is a 'baptism
after which no one sins any more'.[4] But though the old teaching
is gone, Cyprian writes as if determined not to be outdone in
exaltation of martyrdom. In contrast to the first baptism
received for the remission of sins, the second is a baptism
'greater in grace, more lofty in power, more precious in honour,
a baptism wherein angels baptize, . . . a baptism which com-

D

pletes the growth of our faith, a baptism which, as we withdraw
from the world, joins us immediately to God'.[5] The significance
in the change from Tertullian's teaching will become apparent
below; Cyprian had found other means for the forgiveness
of post-baptismal sins.

In other respects also Cyprian moves along paths already
trodden by his African predecessor. The conclusion is inescapable that as the bishop wrote his treatise *de bono Patientiae*
he had Tertullian's work on the same subject at his side and
very often looked at it, so closely do the order of topics and the
ideas correspond. The central theme in both works is identical:
how to hold together the vivid eschatological hope of God's
victory over the world with complete renunciation of the tactics by which the world gains one victory after another over
God's people.

Likewise do we find in Cyprian a pervasive presence of legal
conceptions. Occasion will offer itself below to notice further
instances and developments, but here we may take note of the
prominent idea of 'satisfaction'. According to a very ancient
idea in Roman law a delinquent debtor could be chopped into
pieces by his creditors.[6] By the time of Tertullian and Cyprian
this awesome punishment had been revised so as to allow only
for confiscation of property belonging to the debtor, that is,
unless some alternative means of making good, some 'satisfaction', acceptable to the creditor could be agreed upon.
Tertullian had spoken of satisfaction in two contexts: 1. The
Christian who after his baptism has transgressed the law of
God and thus become God's 'debtor' may undertake the
discipline of second repentance as a satisfaction and thus ward
off the divine wrath at the day of judgement;[7] 2. In a striking
foreshadowing of the later developed doctrine of original sin,
Tertullian writes that fasting undertaken by men today is a
means of making satisfaction to God for Adam's 'primordial
transgression' in eating the fruit of the forbidden tree.[8] Sin,
on this understanding, of course, has become 'crime', 'transgression' of the law of God. Cyprian now develops the theory
of satisfaction in such a way that not only are fasting, penitence,
and prayer itself to be regarded as 'satisfaction' for sin, but
the giving of alms to the poor as well. 'Souls are delivered
from death by almsgiving'; almsgiving is one of the 'remedies

for propitiating God'; fasting and prayer are of little avail without alms for those able to give them;[9] it is even argued, in reflection of the growing practice of infant baptism, that parents may and ought to give alms on behalf of their children.[10]

It would be misleading to suggest that Roman legal conceptions are the sole source of this whole doctrine of satisfaction, which was to have such a long development in Western Catholicism. Although it is not to our purpose here to examine the matter, there can be no doubt that the Catholic doctrine of almsgiving as a means of regaining favour with God is a doctrine which historically owes much to Judaism. Tertullian and Cyprian would agree whole-heartedly that the Church is 'true Israel'. But they were well aware of Judaism, in their own African vicinity, grown from the same stock as the Church, itself dedicated to life in accord with the law of God, and offering in its eschatological hope and in its opposition to idolatry an important alternative to the Church. Cyprian thought it worth his while to compile two books of scriptural *Testimonia* against the Jews, in which his two major themes are that Scripture itself foretells the rejection of the Jews as God's chosen people and that Jesus is the long awaited Messiah. Tertullian had written a book *adversus Judaeos* with like intent. To return to our theme above, Roman law provided both a vocabulary and an 'atmosphere' for the stating of a doctrine of almsgiving as 'satisfaction' whose fundamental content is Jewish in origin.

One would seriously distort if one were to leave the impression that the doctrine of almsgiving as satisfaction were simply an item of teaching which Cyprian the moral theologian felt moved to formulate as he contemplated the services which Roman law and Judaism could render to Christian thought and practice. The stating of this doctrine was worked out in the pastorate of a bishop who cared deeply for the misery of his people, afflicted by plague and famine. He had, we are told by St Jerome, given all his personal fortune to the poor on the occasion of his conversion to the faith. As bishop he was manifestly affected by the contrast between rich and poor in his own congregation and by the blindness of the rich to the need of the poor.[11] The wealthy Christian can be at least as munificent as the wealthy pagan who lavishes his fortune upon a spectacle for the delight of the public; though the pagan can glow in the presence of proconsuls and emperors seated in the boxes, the Christian donor can know that God and Christ look on with delight as he lavishes his spectacle of alms upon the poor.[12] Cyprian's doctrine was an emphatic way of informing the miserly rich of their Christian duty.

It has seemed necessary to dwell a bit upon the above aspects of Cyprian's thought and career. He would himself have been surprised and probably not a little dismayed at the way in which historians and theologians of a later day have abstracted his 'doctrine of the Church' from the broader context of his writings as a whole. Our point has been to emphasize and to illustrate the way in which his thought about the Church fits into a tradition inaugurated by Tertullian. Some chief marks of this tradition are its thoroughly eschatological orientation, its exaltation of martyrdom, its attention to the twin themes of idolatry and the state, and its articulation of the character of Christian life in the language of Roman law. The ecclesiology of our textbooks is a science invented by neither Tertullian nor Cyprian.

Three sets of events occurring during the episcopate of Cyprian are of importance for our understanding of the development of his more narrowly ecclesiological thought. We shall summarize the first of these now, saving the third until later. When the application of the edicts of Decius fell upon the province of Africa, Cyprian left the city of Carthage and retired into a retreat the location of which is not known. The fact of his doing this has given rise to attitudes varying from puzzlement to scandal in the minds both of some Christian contemporaries of Cyprian and of later historians. The option of 'fleeing in time of persecution' had been firmly established in the African Church well before Cyprian, as is evident from two of Tertullian's Catholic books.[13] The option can, after all, claim some support from the New Testament.[14] Cyprian, who was to go to his own martyrdom with no hesitation only a few years hence, lets us gather from his letters that at the time of his retreat the populace were crying out that he should be cast to the lions and that he in fact believed his own retirement from the city to be a means of assisting the safety of others. To have stayed at his post would have been to provide a focus for public rioting, to offer a centre for attack.[15]

One might still wish to remark as follows: In view of the 'ideology' of martyrdom to which we called attention in this chapter and the last, it seems strange to find Cyprian concerned over the possibility of large-scale, indiscriminate attack upon the Church. If one assumes that the man acted and wrote in the fullest integrity, is he none the less not implicitly giving expression to a sense that the Church-in-the-world has more of a future than a literal interpretation of his eschatological hope would suggest? The point may be conceded. But precisely this duality, of intense eschatological belief and a sense of the Church as a structured community with a future in the world, is characteristic of the tradition of thought which it is the task of these chapters to examine. Cyprian had not yet reached the higher gnosis of the twentieth century, whereby he would have been permitted to demythologize his belief concerning the last things. Perhaps if he had, he would not have gone to his martyrdom with such equanimity.

The Decian persecution uncovered the fact that enthusiasm for martyrdom was not so firmly rooted in the Church of Carthage at large as it was in her better remembered representatives. It appears from Cyprian's own words that probably the greater number of Christians did not stand the test.[16] Those who did not followed one of two courses. Some performed the required sacrifices and thus in the eyes of the faithful had 'fallen', 'lapsed'; they were called *lapsi*. Others, among them some of the more wealthy with friends in the imperial administration, succeeded by one or another means in gaining immunity from the necessity to sacrifice through written statements, certificates, passed between themselves and the imperial officers. Such certificates were probably varied in nature, some saying that a sacrifice offered by another person (a pagan friend or slave?) was acceptable evidence of conformity, others denying outright that the person in question was a Christian and implying or stating that he had been in the habit of offering sacrifices, and the like. Thus we have a class of Christians, avoiding sacrifice, called *libellatici*, those who have trafficked in certificates. There was a tendency in the early months of the crisis to regard the *libellatici* as having committed sin equal to that of the *lapsi*, though later their guilt was, at least by Cyprian and his party, accounted less.[17]

Cyprian from his hiding place was in touch with his people and clergy by frequent letters. He received news early on that numbers of the lapsed had visited martyrs in the prisons and had procured from the martyrs written statements forgiving their lapse and declaring that they should be readmitted to the peace and communion of the Church. A group of presbyters in the church of Carthage were willing to honour these papers from the martyrs. The presbyters were probably variously motivated, partly from the traditional respect accorded to the martyrs which we noticed in the first chapter, partly from an old grudge against Cyprian's election as bishop.[18] This party, under the leadership of one Felicissimus, honouring the martyrs and receiving back into communion such of the lapsed as had received papers from the martyrs, soon knew that, even while Cyprian was in hiding, they had to contend with his determined opposition. After the persecution had subsided, Cyprian, back with his people, summoned a council of African bishops to deal with matters pertaining to the lapsed and was successful in carrying the day against the party of Felicissimus. These dissident clergy, after further tactics for gaining recognition of their cause, became the leaders of a schismatic church in Carthage with their own bishop.

The aftermath of the persecution brought division also to the Church at Rome. The bishop Fabian had died as a martyr. After peace had returned, and after the Roman Church had been for over a year without a bishop, Cornelius was elected, much to the chagrin of a leading and very able presbyter, Novatian. Disgruntled, Novatian held views on the subject of the lapsed which were like those of the Catholic Tertullian and also strikingly like those which Cyprian held even up to the point when the latter came out of hiding:[19] there are certain sins, prominent among which is that of idolatry, which are to be accounted sins 'against God', as opposed to lesser offences 'against man', and those who commit such sins after Christian baptism can only submit to penitential discipline and be left to the mercy of God; sins 'against God' cannot be forgiven in the Church or by the Church. The Novatianists were not rigorists on all the old points as the Montanist Tertullian had been, however. Their position as Roman conservatives in the mid-third century is seen from the fact that in accord with the policy of Callistus, inaugurated about the year 220, they readmitted Christians guilty of sexual offence.[20]

The striking difference between Novatian and Cyprian with respect to the lapsed is that whereas Cyprian modified his views to meet the pressure of events, Novatian held to his. Novatian became the bishop of a rival church in Rome and sent representatives to obtain recognition for himself and his church among the Africans, thinking that he could rely upon Cyprian as sharing his views. When this recognition was not won, a Novatianist church with its bishop was formed at Carthage. Thus by the year 252 Cyprian and his Catholic congregation were faced in their city with two rival churches each with its bishop, one receiving lapsed Christians immediately and fully to its fold on the authority of the martyrs, the other refusing to grant peace to the lapsed at all on the ground of their having committed a sin 'against God' unforgivable by the Church.

Cyprian's own position moved to increasing degrees of leniency punctuated by a temporary hardening after his return to the city. His treatise, de Lapsis, written probably as an address to be delivered at the opening of the council of bishops in 251, has in mind only the traditional penitential discipline, with ultimate forgiveness by God alone,[21] a position essentially identical with that of Tertullian's Catholic treatise, de Poenitentia. Here he expresses a notable stiffness over against the martyrs. No one is to cry down their dignity, their glories, and their crowns; but the martyrs may not order something to be done in the Church which is against the words of the gospel, and the Lord himself had expressly declared, 'He who denies me, him will I also deny.'[22] The merits of the martyrs will indeed be of avail with the Judge, but only at the last day.[23] The occasional ambiguity with which he expresses himself in this address, however, makes his further moves not incomprehensible.

In fact this ambiguity also points back to some preliminary decisions which he had reached in concealment and had communicated to the church. And here, first off, is one of the nice ironies in this course of events. Novatian, writing to Cyprian in the name of the Roman clergy then without a

bishop, had revealed in the most circumspect and hesitant
fashion that lapsed Christians, giving ample evidences of their
penitence, and in the interim before the election of a new
bishop in Rome, were being received to the peace of the Church
on their deathbed.[24] Novatian himself, therefore, is clearly
party to a decision in the direction of leniency in the days
before his rigorist schism. Cyprian took up the suggestion but
was not willing to be quite as lenient as Novatian and the
Roman clergy. The lapsed, in addition to being penitent
and on their deathbed, were to have certificates from the
martyrs.[25]

Thus from an initial move which if anything was more
conservative than that reported by Novatian, Cyprian gradually
abandoned his original view of the demands of 'evangelical
vigour'. As he says, he 'yielded to the necessity of the times'.[26]
Still in concealment he directed that some who had once sacrificed but afterwards had publicly confessed the name of Christ
and were being sent into exile, should be received to communion.[27] The assembled bishops at the council in 251 determined that the *libellatici* should be admitted but that those who
had actually sacrificed must undertake the traditional penance
and would be admitted on their deathbed.[28] Some two years
later we find him recommending that those who had sacrificed
only after severe torture be admitted to communion after a
penance of three years' duration.[29] With the resumption of
persecution in the spring of 253 he became persuaded that
reception of the Eucharist in the peace of the Church was the
best kind of armour for the new contest, and so in common with
his fellow bishops, decided to admit all of those who had sacrificed and who had thereafter continuously done penance.[30]
And finally, in a letter in which he *may* be exaggerating a bit
for the sake of impressing his leniency upon his correspondent,
Cornelius of Rome, we see him commenting that he remits
all sins, even all those committed against God, to those who
come in humble confession.[31]

The implications for Cyprian's doctrine of the Church in
these changes in penitential policy will be explored below.
We shall see also that he did not abandon every kind of rigour.
But a point which must be made immediately is that Cyprian
did not see the essential difference between himself and the two

rival bishops at Carthage, nor the difference between Cornelius and Novatian at Rome, as a difference among policies in treating the problem of the lapsed. Though such differences gave him much pain, Cyprian, when he came right down to it, was willing to tolerate them among Catholic bishops.[32] Cyprian's cause for offence was rather that his rivals at Carthage, and Novatian at Rome, were not *Catholic* bishops. They had departed from the unity of the Church.

For our purposes here the most useful and illuminating way in which to view Cyprian's conception of the unity of the Church is to see it as a striking development of the conception of the Church as an alternative, a substitute, society to that of the Roman empire. Within this conception the idea of law is prominent. We saw this theme being sounded clearly by Tertullian. In Tertullian the language of law, so far as the empirical Church is concerned, is drawn largely from the body of civil and criminal law, i.e. the laws regulating relations among individuals and groups, and those having to do with transgressors of the law. The farthest point, on the whole, that a constitutional conception of the Church reached with Tertullian was in his designation of the *local* church as composed of clergy and people on the model of *ordo* and *plebs*. In his view of the succession of bishops is to be seen a fusion of the civil-law concept of succession in possession with a rather different notion, that of the head teachers in the two major schools of jurisprudence as 'succeeding' one another.

In Cyprian we see the logic of Tertullian's basic conception being applied on a much larger scale. Cyprian considers the entire Church Catholic in constitutional terms. It is of course true that the language of constitutional law is already present in Tertullian, but it is present largely in his conception of God and of God's relation to the world. The Church, in the end, for Tertullian is made up of 'bodies', however small, who can claim possession of the Spirit; for him, so long as the Spirit is present in unmistakable power, the Church is thereby constituted. For Cyprian such a conception as this would do nothing but make nonsense of the idea of a 'Catholic' Church. It is symptomatic of Cyprian's shifting of gears at this point that whereas he, from the beginning of his writings concerning the Novatianist problem onwards, speaks repeatedly of the

'Catholic Church', there is no sure evidence that Tertullian had even used that formula. The Church as an object of reflection attains a new kind of significance in Cyprian. Our provisional thesis here is, then, that while denying some of Tertullian's most striking conclusions regarding the Church, Cyprian expands and applies at a new level a logic which he found in that author.

For those who had the interests of the Roman empire at heart, the health of the empire was indissolubly linked to the notions of 'peace and concord'; these ends in turn were unattainable apart from a universal compliance with law in whose administration the provincial governors were key figures. This is the model which Cyprian takes. The Church is a universal society founded upon law which it is the business of the Church's own governors to administer.

Behind the divinely appointed provisions for the governance of the Church stand the more ultimate ends of 'peace and concord': the peace and concord of Christ.[33] The Church as a universal society has been constituted by the law of God. That law has placed bishops in the role of the Church's 'governors', and 'every act of the Church is ruled by these very governors'.[34] Just as the provinces of the empire each had its 'council of the province' to which went delegates from the cities to discuss matters of common interest, so do Cyprian's bishops come regularly from their towns and cities to debate and to decide in council upon issues of present concern. Each bishop in his own time and at his own place is a 'judge in place of Christ',[35] which is to say that the bishop is a magistrate having plenipotentiary authority from Christ the judge. It is bishops, therefore, who in fact have authority to regulate and to modulate the Church's penitential requirements, and to decide individual cases on their merits.[36]

Cyprian did not believe that in saying such things he was operating in the realm of theory and speculation. The authority of bishops is founded upon express words of Christ to the Apostles. In the sixteenth chapter of Matthew the Lord had given to Peter the keys of the kingdom of heaven, declaring that whatever he loosed and bound on earth would be loosed and bound in heaven, and in the twenty-first chapter of John he had given the same authority to all the Apostles. In this regard Cyprian took a crucial step in the history of thought about the episcopate: the Apostles themselves were the first bishops of the Church.[37]

The logic of the matter must have seemed fairly clear to Cyprian. To the Apostles was given the judicial authority of binding and loosing. The doctrine of apostolic succession had been formulated by Irenaeus and Tertullian as a way of establishing the authority of the rule of faith. That battle had been won by Cyprian's day at least so far as the Catholic Church was concerned. Now the problem was not doctrinal, in the sense that it did not have to do directly with the fundamental proclamation of the Church as enshrined in the rule of faith. The problem now was a disciplinary one; it had to do with decisions regarding lapse into idolatry and readmission to fellowship, decisions, moreover, affecting large numbers of people. The doctrine of apostolic succession lay at hand, and a fairly obvious relevance was easily discovered in the precise words of Jesus to the Apostles giving them authority over binding and loosing, the forgiving and retaining of sins. But, as we said, it was precisely to the Apostles that this authority was given. A pressing necessity for bishops to act as Church magistrates has now arisen; upon the Apostles was bestowed judicial authority; the Apostles, then, were the first bishops.

Furthermore, Cyprian did not himself simply invent the notion that a bishop is a kind of judge exercising disciplinary authority. Callistus of Rome had taken the important step of admitting adulterers back to the Church's communion, and African bishops before Cyprian had acted in accord with this policy. Cyprian was aware that this change had taken place in Africa and approved it.[38] Cyprian entered the episcopate, therefore, in a context in which bishops already exercised a kind of judicial authority which he now formally attributes to them and which he sees as having been given to the Apostles. It was no overweening lust for either authority or honour that led Cyprian to designate the Apostles as bishops; and thereby it was also natural to discover a new meaning in the succession of bishops, since the Romans spoke of their governors, each of whom was chief magistrate in his province, as 'succeeding' one another.

The bishops are successors to the Apostles. In one of Cyprian's most famous phrases, bishops succeed the Apostles *vicaria ordinatione*. This is language drawn from the vocabulary of imperial administration designating the kind of authority which an officeholder possesses relative to some prior or higher official. To say that bishops succeed to the Apostles in this way is to say that they possess their office 'by appointment with fully delegated power'. When Christ, therefore, declared to the Apostles, 'He that hears you, hears me', he was speaking to the first bishops of the Church and to all future bishops.[39] Lightly to engage in calumny of a bishop is to make oneself a judge of God and of Christ, who have delivered to bishops their awesome authority in the Church.[40]

Christ in a very special way appointed the episcopate to rule the Church. So far as we have yet seen, the episcopate might have appeared simply to be an aggregate, Tertullian's 'number of bishops', each one autonomous and isolated in possession of his office by succession from the Apostles. In this case the model provided by the state would seem to break down; the provincial governors, after all, did not exercise their office autonomously; they were there on commission from the emperor. The model does in fact break down, because for Cyprian there is no human officer in the Church parallel to the emperor. This fact, however, is not simply a token of the breaking down of a model. It is in part also a token of a certain tension between an older and a newer model. The old concept of Roman judicial authority, reaching even into the third century A.D., was tied closely to the handing over of such authority from one magistrate to his successor. Imperial despotism might increasingly erode the practical significance of this idea, but theoretically the empire was erected upon just such venerable institutions as this. For Cyprian that which makes him and his episcopal colleagues something more than a 'number of bishops' is to be found in his new conception of 'episcopate' and in the significance which he attaches to the figure of Peter in the sixteenth chapter of Matthew. Peter is the rock upon whom Christ says that he builds his Church, and it is to Peter that he entrusts the authority of binding and loosing. In the twentieth chapter of John he gives identical authority to all the Apostles in stating that the sins

which they remit are remitted, and the sins which they retain
are retained. It is clear, thinks Cyprian, that all the Apostles
possess identical authority. The passage from John records
words spoken after the resurrection of Jesus, and the passage
from Matthew words spoken before the resurrection. The significance of Jesus' having entrusted authority to Peter at a
prior time lies in his intention to demonstrate at the outset
the unity of the episcopate, the unity of the episcopal office.
To use Cyprian's own words from his treatise, *de Catholicae
Ecclesiae Unitate,*

> . . . that he might make clear the unity, he by his authority
> established the origin of that very unity as beginning from
> one Apostle. Certainly the other Apostles were also the
> same as was Peter, endowed with an equal partnership both
> of honour and of power, but the beginning proceeds from
> unity, so that the Church of Christ may be shown to be one.[41]

On this basis it is not only the Church that is one but the
episcopate as well, the episcopate understood as a teaching,
judicial, and priestly office. The episcopate is one *cathedra*,
one teaching office.[42] The several bishops constitute a *corpus*,
that is to say a legal corporation, whose 'property' the episcopate, one might say, is held in common among them.[43] Every
bishop possesses the whole of the authority of the episcopate
in his own place, a notion to which Cyprian gives expression
in one of his densest, most cryptic, and most famous sentences:
'The episcopate is one, the local exercise of which is held
by single bishops each with the authority of the whole.'[44]
The body of bishops together form a 'college', a college of
'co-priests' (*consacerdotes*), whose business it is to be in 'concord'
with one another.[45] Just as the body of the Church itself
exists throughout the world in its many members, so the body
of the episcopate is diffused among a harmonious multitude of
bishops.[46]

It will have been noticed that the words with which Jesus
founded the episcopate are also the words with which he
founded the Church. The Church is 'constituted' upon the
bishops. The point has two related consequences, one more
practical and the other more theoretical. At the practical and

empirical level it means that the Church in any given place is that flock of people united to its Catholic pastor the bishop. 'The bishop is in the Church and the Church in the bishop,' and anyone not with the bishop is not in the Church.[47] Once a bishop has been placed in his office by vote of the clergy, 'suffrage of the people', and ordination by other Catholic bishops, it is simply impossible that there be another and rival Catholic bishop in that place. That Novatian acted out of accord with this principle is Cyprian's fundamental complaint against him; by his schism Novatian has placed himself outside the unity of the Church and can no more be called a Christian.[48] In speaking of those in Africa claiming peace for the lapsed on the authority of the martyrs, Cyprian uses strikingly political language: 'And then the beginning of this insurrection began to take place. In our province, throughout a number of cities, an attack has been made by the crowd upon their rulers.'[49] Their error has been to act without the authority of the bishop, and to them must be said: 'He cannot have God for his father who does not have the Church for his mother.'[50] Even the death of a martyr outside the unity of the Church is not a Christian martyrdom; 'there is no salvation outside the Church'. In expressing himself on the martyrs Cyprian unmistakably carries on the Tertullianic motif of continuity between the Church here and now and the Church of the kingdom to come: 'He cannot be a martyr who is not in the Church; he cannot attain to the kingdom who forsakes the Church that will rule there.'[51]

The more theoretical application of Cyprian's principle has to do with another aspect of his relation to Tertullian. It has often been noted that Cyprian is emphatic in relating his insistence upon the unity of the Church to the unity of God. This is true enough, so far as it goes.[52] But Cyprian allows us to gather rather more precisely what this association of ideas means to him. We have noted above that for the discussion of theological matters Tertullian notably turns to the language of constitutional law only when he is putting forward a doctrine of God and of God's relation to the world. He urges in the third chapter of *adversus Praxean* that a doctrine of Trinity does not destroy God's 'monarchy', God's single rule of the world, any more than the single rule of an empire is necessarily destroyed either by the sharing of the emperor's rule with his son or by the provincial governors and a host of other officials acting under the emperor.[53]

Now it appears that Cyprian in the fifth chapter of his work *de Catholicae Ecclesiae Unitate* is wanting to make an analogous point. He announces first his theme that the episcopate is one and undivided, each bishop possessing the whole of its authority, and then sounds immediately and briefly the twin theme of the unity of the Church. These remarks are followed by three similes of unity in multiplicity which are subsequently applied generally to the Church. But this application of the similes to the Church is preceded by words which attempt not so much to analogize the Church's unity in multiplicity as to turn the similes to another use: to warn against separation from the Catholic Church with its episcopate. It is worth our while to quote the entire passage:

> The episcopate is one, the local exercise of which is held by single bishops each with the authority of the whole. The Church is one, which by abundant increase is spread widely abroad into a multitude, as there are many rays of the sun, but one light; and many branches of a tree but one trunk bound fast to its roots; and although from one spring flow many streams, and though a great number of them seem to be poured forth in the largesse of a gushing abundance, yet their oneness is preserved in their origin. Separate a ray of the sun from the sun's body; the unity between the sun and ray does not permit such a division of light. Break a branch from the tree: when broken it will not be able to bud. Cut off the stream from its source: when cut off it dries up. Thus also the Church, bathed in the light of the Lord, shoots out her rays through the whole world; but it is one light which is everywhere diffused, and the unity of the body is not severed. Her rich fertility spreads her branches over the entire earth. She expands generously and broadly her free flowing streams. Yet her headspring is one and her origin one; and she is one mother, plenteous in the happy fruits of her fecundity. Of her womb we are born; by her milk we are nourished; by her spirit we are animated.[54]

The one most likely source from which Cyprian could have

drawn these similes of unity in multiplicity is the eighth chapter of Tertullian's treatise *adversus Praxean*. There the images of the ray from the sun, the river flowing from its spring, and the shoot growing from its root are employed to illustrate the unity in plurality of the divine Trinity, the three persons of which share the divine monarchy over the world.

Cyprian makes clear reference to the episcopate in the above explication of his similes. When he speaks elsewhere of the 'root', 'origin', and 'matrix' of the Church, it is not always clear whether he means the Catholic Church as such or the episcopate in particular, and indeed the distinction for him would be unreal, the one is unthinkable without the other; the constituting of the episcopate is the constituting of the Church; the initial constituting of the episcopate in Peter sets forth the 'origin' both of the episcopate and of the Church.[55] The whole of chapters 4–6, from the middle of which the above extract is taken, moves around two points: the unity of the Church under and with the episcopate, and the unity of the episcopate as shared among its many members.

Our conclusions, then, are threefold:

1. The Trinitarian images of unity in multiplicity are here applied explicitly to the relation between the episcopate and the Church.

2. Cyprian appears to be groping towards a further application of the Trinitarian similes which he does not explicitly formulate.

3. This second application, only dimly adumbrated, but, I think, really adumbrated, might be formulated as follows: the Trinitarian images, images by which the 'monarchy' of the three divine persons is to be made intelligible, may be seen as suggesting the way in which the members of the episcopate share an undivided rule over the Church. The episcopate arises from 'one', just as does the triune godhead. The plausibility of this conjecture follows from the way in which the unity of the episcopate and the unity of the Church are two themes which move in tandem throughout this whole section of Cyprian's book, and from the fact that they are explicitly announced one after the other immediately before mention of the Trinitarian similes. Thus would Cyprian's political model of the Church be brought to a kind of completion with the

aid of Tertullian's language concerning the rule of the divine monarchy over the world.

Cyprian's total conception of the nature of the Church and of the Church's unity must be the final criterion of the meaning of the word 'Catholic' in his vocabulary. Much print has been expended over the question whether by this word he meant to signify chiefly the Church's universality in a geographical sense or the Church's unity under the divinely instituted episcopate. He never gives in so many words a definition to the term; its meaning must be gathered from his usage. There can be no doubt as to the denotation of the term: the Catholic Church is the Church which has preserved its identity as the Church founded upon and bound in unity to the episcopate, the Church ruled by bishops each of whom holds his office through regular election of the local church and through ordination by bishops who trace the line of their ordination to the Apostles, the Church whose bishops have never been stained by the sin either of idolatry or of schism. As to the connotation of the term one must perforce be more speculative. To call the Church 'Catholic', it seems, is to say that the Church has held fast to its integrity in the senses just specified; it is to say that the Church has rested fast in its wholeness, a wholeness which has been neither rent apart by schism nor corrupted by the guilt of its bishops. This Church is indeed spread abroad geographically through many widely scattered places, but there appears no good reason to assert that for this author 'Catholic' is intended to signify 'universal' in that geographical sense.[56]

It should now be clear that Cyprian, under the pressure of events related to two waves of persecution, formulated a doctrine of the Church which is certainly not that of Tertullian but which goes further upon a way of conceiving the Church which the earlier writer had laid down. We have now to ask what further differences have come about as the result of Cyprian's combined teaching and practice stated above. Two such immediately appear.

First, Cyprian has had in some measure to give up the idea of the Church as composed of saints who since their baptism have not fallen into sin 'against God'. Well before the end of

E

his career he had readmitted to communion those who had performed pagan sacrifices. We have seen him writing that he remits 'all things' to those who come in penitent confession of their sin. He takes the crucially important step of admitting and stating explicitly that there are 'tares' in the Church. The Lord's parable of the wheat and the tares growing together in the same field is a parable about the Church. The words of the Apostle concerning vessels of various degrees of worth in one great house, some for 'honourable' and some for 'ignoble' use, are words about the Church. Likewise with the parable of the lost sheep.[57] This immediately means that the judgement of God will be a somewhat more complicated affair than Tertullian had imagined. It also means for Cyprian that forgiveness and readmission to the communion of the Church at the hands of a bishop are not necessarily any assurance of coming out on top at the last day. Cyprian, the old rigorist, is not at all confident that those whom he has readmitted will not have to face the divine wrath, and Cyprian the pastor is well aware that his large-scale practice of readmission has in the case of some simply been the occasion of their falling into even worse depravity.[58] The final day of judgement, therefore, will not simply be an occasion when the Church is once and for all separated from the world. The judgement of God will break into the Church itself. 'The Lord who is coming to his Church will without question judge those whom he will find in it.'[59]

From Cyprian's vantage point after many months of repeated and agonizing reappraisal, it seems nonsense to require acts of penitence from those genuinely penitent without in the end giving them the 'fruit' of their acts of satisfaction, since it is evident from Scripture that God does not deny pardon to sinners. The presence of forgiven sinners in the Church does not bring about the pollution of the Church as a whole, since Scripture is equally clear that every man is held responsible only for his own sin; 'it is not possible for one man to become guilty for another'.[60]

And Cyprian does in fact put forward precisely the legal argument which Tertullian had foreseen as the consequence of the readmission of adulterers. Adulterers have committed sin 'by will'. Crimes committed 'by will' are much more serious before the law than those committed 'by necessity', 'by compulsion'. Here there are two different applications of the notion of 'necessity'. On the one hand it applies to those who have performed pagan sacrifices after prolonged torture.[61] On the other it applies to those who have ignorantly supposed that in securing a certificate of sacrifice from the authorities they have done nothing reprehensible; Cyprian appears to know of cases in which, for example, a man has been told by his bishop that the one act to be avoided above all others is that of sacrificing and that to secure a certificate is to do nothing more than to pay a fine for the privilege of refraining from an act forbidden to Christians.[62] We have here the implicit argument that to commit a crime in ignorance of its gravity is to be guilty of it only in a very attenuated sense; it is to sin 'by necessity'.

There is a certain irony in the fact that the more rigorous Cyprian, who wrote the work *de Lapsis* soon after emerging from retirement, can there use an argument similar but not quite identical to that which he will use to support his more 'relaxed' policy. Cyprian the rigorist argues that only God can pardon sins committed 'against himself' and on this basis justifies a lifelong period of penitence for the lapsed. Cyprian the more chastened pastor urges that it is only the Lord who can be the stern judge of those same sins. In defence of both policies he cites the scriptural text: 'A servant is not greater than his lord.'[63]

In short, we observe a twofold process at work in Cyprian's mind: the *judgement* of God as operating to separate wheat from tares within the Church becomes an increasingly real possibility and is increasingly left to him alone; the *mercy* of God to forgive sinners becomes increasingly a policy governing the Church's attitude to those within her midst.

It would be a simple matter if with that we could leave the problem of Cyprian's rigorism. But we cannot. The radical, primitive doctrine of the eschatological purity and holiness of the Church has still a very strong hold on him; one might even say, distorting a bit, that in fact it has not lost any of its hold on him.

In one of his early letters, written from his hiding place to the lapsed who were claiming the peace of the Church on the authority of the martyrs, Cyprian wrote: 'I marvel that some, with daring audacity, have chosen to write to me as if they wrote in the name of the Church, when the Church is constituted in the bishop, the clergy, and all those who stand fast in the faith.'[64] The later clause of this sentence is no mere emphatic rhetoric. There is present in the developing thought of Cyprian a problem of consistency which is nowhere brought clearly to the surface and nowhere clearly acknowledged, not to speak of its being resolved. Implicit in the above quotation is the thought that the Church in the legal sense, which for Cyprian is the supremely important sense, has its existence in the bishop, clergy, and those who continue steadfast, not yielding to idolatry. This means, in the light of what we have now seen of Cyprian's developing thought, that those who lapse and are then readmitted to full fellowship are indeed 'in the Church' in some sense but in a sense that is never really specified. We have seen above that the founding of the episcopate and the founding of the Church occur in one and the same action of Jesus; the founding of the Church is in fact the founding of the episcopate. The result of this construction of the matter in Cyprian's evolving thought is that bishops, in order to be and remain bishops of the Catholic Church, must remain free of serious sins. It is upon the bishops personally that falls the burden of retaining the Church's eschatological holiness.

Cyprian develops this theme in relation to the Bishop's office as 'priest'. To the aid of his thought come both Roman notions of the ceremonial purity requisite for the performance of priestly offices as well as the use of the Old Testament as an authentic source of Christian law. The bishop is a priest (*sacerdos*). In his offering of the eucharistic sacrifice he acts 'in the place of Christ'; he 'imitates' what was done in Christ's own offering of himself to the Father.[65] For the exercise of such an office Cyprian reckons that a man must be 'unstained and ceremonially pure'.[66] To him apply the Levitical prescriptions governing the exercise of priesthood: 'The man in whom there is spot or blemish shall not approach to offer gifts to God.'[67] Both the offering of pagan sacrifice and the acquiring of certificates of sacrifice disqualify a man from holding the episcopal office. If a bishop has been found guilty of one of these sins he can continue in the Church only as a layman after a period of penance. And the same liability falls upon a bishop who has led his people into schism and thereafter returns to the Church.[68] The act of attempting to sever the Church's unity, therefore, is an act equal in its effects to the act of idolatry. A schismatic bishop has erected a 'profane altar', has set up an 'adulterous throne', and offers 'sacrilegious sacrifices'.[69]

It bears emphasizing that Cyprian's discussion of all of these problems is conducted with an eschatological urgency. Just as the coming of persecution upon the Church is a sign of the approach of Antichrist, who will precede the appearance of the avenging Lord, so is the schism at Carthage such a sign, so Novatian's schism at Rome, and so the turmoil in the Church over bishops who have lapsed.[70]

In the above ways does Cyprian in his latter days see himself as upholding 'the vigour of the gospel'. The eschatological purity of the whole Church has become a sacral purity attaching to her bishops.

The absence of coherence of which we spoke above shows itself in Cyprian's contrary views upon the effect which a man's sin has upon those with whom he is in communion in the Church. Whereas in arguing for the readmission of lapsed laymen he urged that a man is held fast only in his own sins and cannot be guilty for the sin of another, in the case of lapsed or of schismatic bishops he appeals to the notion of ceremonial contagion, or infection, a notion which he had taken the trouble explicitly to repudiate in the case of laymen.

Perhaps we are being too unfriendly and taking an insufficiently historical view in speaking of an absence of coherence. In Cyprian's mind the matter probably seemed relatively clear: the bishop's priestly office as such makes him liable to certain sacral, legal requirements which do not apply to the laity. A bishop who lapses from these requirements has, with respect to the exercise of his episcopal office, been contaminated, stained, and to all people with whom he holds communion he spreads the contagion of his sin. It is of the utmost urgency that Christians, both laypeople and bishops, withdraw from communion with bishops so stained. 'All are absolutely bound tight to sin who have been contaminated by the sacrifice of a profane and unrighteous priest.'[71] If Christians find that their own bishop has been guilty of the kind of lapse here in question, it is their manifest duty to separate themselves from him and choose another bishop.[72] The clear and emphatic teaching of Cyprian in this matter was to make an ominous contribution to the history of Christianity in Africa, as we shall see in the next chapter.

Stephen, bishop of Rome from 254 to 257, came to the Roman episcopate when the Novatianist schism was already three years old. The Novatianist Church had engaged in its own missionary expansion and, of course, had baptized its converts. The question then arose as to how to receive such people if and when they chose to leave the Novatianist and enter the Catholic Church. Stephen's decision was that they should not again undergo baptism in water but that the bishop should receive them by laying his hand upon them. The question as to who had been the minister of baptism is irrelevant, baptism deriving its effect not from its administrant but from the 'majesty of the name' of Jesus Christ and from the faith of the one who is baptized.[73] Stephen defended his policy as being in accord with the ancient and continuous practice of the Roman Church, even reaching, apparently, to that Church's practice in receiving Marcionites.[74]

The question arises as to the meaning of the laying-on of the bishop's hand. The evidence is not entirely clear and must be gathered from Cyprian's correspondence. It appears that Stephen and the Roman clergy adopted two lines of interpretation at one or another time. On the one hand the imposition of the bishop's hand was seen as an analogy to the practice whereby Christians who had committed post-baptismal sin were received to the Church's communion after evidence of their penitence.[75] On the other hand the rationale was developed that the bishop was completing the act of initiation begun in water baptism, and in the imposition of his hand was imparting the gift of the Holy Spirit.[76] This theory reflects a further notion, fast gaining ground in the third century, namely, that the rite of Christian initiation is separable into two clearly defined parts, the forgiveness of sins by the bathing in water and the subsequent gift of the Spirit through the imposition of the bishop's hand.[77] On the second rationale, the schismatics administer a valid water baptism, though they do not possess the Spirit and cannot therefore bestow it in their own rite of imposition.[78] Stephen claimed, on the other hand, that in schismatic baptism the believer obtains the 'grace of Christ'.[79] The assumption common to both of these lines of interpretation is that the Spirit of God is not present in schismatic and heretical churches.

Stephen was much incensed by the refusal of Cyprian and the African bishops to follow him in his policy, and adopted a provocative argument for bringing the recalcitrant bishops into line. In the history of the Roman episcopate he was the first, so far as we know, to appeal to his own particular position as successor to Peter on whom the Lord built his Church, the first to claim thereby a 'primacy' entitling him to be obeyed by other bishops.[80] Though many scholars seem reluctant to acknowledge the point, the evidence seems reasonably clear that Stephen declared excommunicate churches whose bishops would not agree to and follow his policy.[81] At the very least there is no reason to doubt that Stephen refused 'peace and communion' to delegates coming to him from Cyprian.[82] After Stephen's death in 257 and Cyprian's martyrdom in 258, the crisis seems carefully to have been ignored though not forgotten, the Africans continuing into the fourth century their practice of baptizing schismatics.

To Cyprian both the practice and the theorizing of Stephen and his party seemed horrible nonsense. In a crucial way it involved the problem of the relation between the Spirit of God and the Church. We have seen this problem already present in the writings of Tertullian. The latter author was forced to a decision, as it were, between the empirical Catholic Church and the manifest working of the Spirit in prophecy, works of healing, and rigorous ethical demand. He chose for the latter. For Cyprian the Catholic bishop there is no alternative posed between Church and Spirit. Again we refer to the words of Jesus instituting both the episcopate and the Church. In the twentieth chapter of John Jesus preceded his commission to the Apostles to forgive and remit sins by 'breathing' on them and saying: 'Receive the Holy Spirit'. From this it followed clearly that the Church of the Catholic episcopate is the place where the Spirit is. There is no other Spirit of God than the Spirit of Catholic unity. The Novatianists, having departed from that unity, do not possess the Spirit. The commissioning of the Apostles to forgive sins was in the first instance a commissioning to baptize. To put the point in legal language, the Novatianists, and all other schismatics, do not have the requisite 'license' to baptize; their baptism is not 'valid', 'legitimate'.[83]

In rebutting arguments put forward by the party of Stephen, Cyprian makes clear that the doctrine of the Spirit is at the heart of the matter. If one claims that schismatic baptism is effective to forgive sins, it is clear from the words of Jesus on the contrary that only they can forgive sins who possess the Spirit.[84] If it is suggested that the gift of the Spirit is given to schismatics when they join themselves to the Catholic Church, the absurdity of this is manifest from the point just made: if the schismatics can forgive sins, for which the Spirit is requisite, then their own rite of the imposition of the bishop's hand will avail for them as well.[85]

It may be noticed in passing that in the course of his argument with Stephen, Cyprian is fighting manfully to uphold the unity of the Christian rite of initiation. The entire rite, including immersion in water and imposition of the bishop's hand, is encompassed by the action of the Spirit. A man cannot be born of God and made holy unless each 'part' of the total rite is present, and present within Catholic unity. 'A part cannot be void and a part valid.'[86]

The only possible conclusion from these considerations is that when schismatics come to the Catholic Church they must be baptized. From Cyprian's point of view it would be quite misleading to speak of 'rebaptism'. That profane and sacrilegious washing which the schismatics purport to administer in the name of Christ is not Christian baptism.

Worth pointing out is a striking similarity between Cyprian's doctrine of baptism and a kind of argument employed by Tertullian which we noticed in the previous chapter. Just as Tertullian can urge a developing body of 'rigorist' ethical prescriptions on the basis of an appeal to 'reason' and 'truth' over against 'custom', so Cyprian can use the same legal argument in the defence of his tight, logical, rigorous doctrine of baptism. Cyprian is not a Catholic to appeal indiscriminately to the unvarying tradition of the universal Church. He never calls into question the claim that Stephen's policy at Rome is in accord with the traditional practice of that Church. His interest only is in the defensibility of that practice. And so he urges that the appeal to 'custom' is in this instance worthless, since those who so appeal are in fact 'demolished by reason'. Custom is not greater than truth.[87] We have here an important tool for the 'development of Christian doctrine', a development which Cyprian implicitly admits taking place.

It remains to take note of a further legacy of Cyprian's writings that was to provide occasion for much subsequent comment, a legacy of another unresolved problem. We return to the theme of harmony and concord announced above. Cyprian was entirely persuaded that 'concord' among the bishops was one of the marks of the Spirit's presence. The crucial question is whether such accord means agreement in theory and practice on important matters of Church discipline and of sacramental administration, or whether it means the preservation of unity in communion among bishops who agree to differ about such matters. Cyprian's letters give evidence of both views, but it is not right to say that one or the other wins out in the end. They both win, in different respects. He writes to Stephen in regard to the bishop of Arles, turned Novatianist, and presses his correspondent to withdraw from communion with the man and to write to Arles directing the people to choose another bishop; at the end of the letter he observes that among those bishops in whom there is the one Spirit there cannot be contrariety of understanding. 'It is manifest that he does not hold the truth of the Holy Spirit with the rest whom we observe to think differently.'[88] In the very depths of despair Cyprian writes of bishops who hold communion with lapsed bishops and sounds the sectarian themes of ceremonial contagion and of withdrawal from all such. 'In matters of this sort there can be no acceptance of a man's standing, neither can human indulgence yield anything to anyone when sacred authority in Scripture interposes and lays down a law.'[89] On the other hand he cites the fact that in the recent history of the African Church there had been disagreement among bishops as to whether adulterers should be readmitted to the Church, and recalls with approval that the disagreeing bishops did not break communion with one another; of that incident he could say that 'the bond of concord remained'.[90] In the interest of the same concord he can with notable equanimity write, in reference to the baptism of schismatics, that he wishes to prescribe nothing to any bishop, that every bishop has the 'free exercise of his own judgement'.[91]

So it depends on what the issue is. If it concerns disciplinary practice concerning laymen and the admission of schismatic laity to the Catholic Church, then the individual bishop, benighted though he may be, is left to his own freedom and to the final judgement of God. If it concerns a bishop who has performed pagan sacrifice and who persists in wanting to remain in his see, there is no question of leaving individual bishops to their own devices; the contagion of a lapsed bishop's sin spreads to all who are in communion with him, whether his own flock or other bishops with their flocks. We encounter again the special and crucially important place of the bishop in Cyprian's scheme.

Cyprian's theology, highly eschatological in its tone, pervaded by the conceptions and language of law, comes to focus directly on the problem of the Church—its unity, its bounds, its function in the purposes of God, and its relation to the Spirit of God. Cyprian the eschatological and rigorist Christian comes to terms with Cyprian the sensitive pastor and man of his times, through a conception such that the Church's bishops are the essential organs of her unity and the essential bearers of her holiness. The tension between unity and holiness, thus understood, was subsequently discovered to be unbearable.

3

THE DONATISTS AND AUGUSTINE:
FORBEARING ONE ANOTHER IN LOVE

The impression is inescapable that while Augustine listened
to what the Donatists said, he had his mind on something
else. It became his problem to bring the heritage of Latin
thought about the Church into adjustment with the new situation created in the fourth century by the establishment of
Christianity as the religion of the empire. He came to this task
after a long intellectual and moral pilgrimage. This personal
journey had finally brought him to Catholic Christianity
after his discovery that Platonist philosophy offered a road upon
which he could begin to solve pressing theoretical problems
having to do with the nature of man, the nature of God,
and the nature of evil. Catholic and Protestant Christianity
to our own day have recorded their debt to Augustine's
intellectual achievement by a long history of explicit and implicit appeal to the thought of the great African doctor. He was
an adventuresome, seminal, and creative theologian whose
horizons were far broader than those either of Latin theology
prior to him or of most Latin Christians contemporary with
him.

In particular Augustine's horizons were not those of the
Donatists. The sensitive reader of today cannot but be aware
of the way in which genuine theological achievement is the
product of those who know that new occasions teach new
duties. But the same reader will sense a certain heartache at the
sight of a great man, with the future on his side and with his
attention firmly fastened on the issues as he sees them, doing
battle with religious folk to whom he does not listen very
carefully.

It cannot be our business here either to give an account of
the history of Donatism or to enter explicitly into current debate

as to the relative roles in the movement's history of religious and theological factors on the one hand and of social, sectional, and political factors on the other. It seems appropriate, however, to state two assumptions underlying the treatment to follow:

1. It would be surprising, though not out of the question, to discover that any social movement expressing itself continuously and explicitly in religious terms can be explained *simply* by reference to non-religious factors.

2. It has not yet been shown that the Donatist movement in particular, either in its origins or in its subsequent history, is to be identified as a movement of poor, rural African nationalists in protest against rich, urban, and Romanized society.

The second of these assumptions is quite compatible with the thesis that social and sectional factors contributed to the dynamic of the movement and even powerfully influenced decisions made by the movement's leaders at crucial junctures. It is a difficult matter, and to do it justice would require a careful statement of the distinction between 'religious factors' and 'social factors'. But such is not for us here. Our concern is with theology, and our view is that theology cannot in this instance be reduced to social ideology.

The Donatist movement proceeded from a deep sense of disturbance among African Christians over the knowledge that a distressing number of their leaders in the episcopate had been disloyal in the great persecution preceding the coming of peace to the Church under the Christian emperor Constantine. In similar fashion to Decius several decades before him, the emperor Diocletian at the end of the third century renewed a policy of restoration with a view to securing the stability and peace of the emperor under the aegis of the gods. To this policy was coupled the emperor's growing sense that Christians in the army and administration were producing both disloyalty in the ranks and the displeasure of the gods. He was thus led to a series of edicts in the years 303–4 directed specifically against the Christians. Churches were to be destroyed, the Christian Scriptures handed over to the authorities for burning, leading clergy arrested and forced to sacrifice, and finally all Christians of whatever rank required to sacrifice as well. The edicts were applied variously and with varying degrees of severity in the different provinces.

In Africa the chief bone of contention, both during and after the persecution, was that of bishops who had or had not handed over the Scriptures to the government. In the wake of the persecution there had emerged by the year 312 a separate church body, with its own bishops, claiming that it was the Catholic Church of Africa, and that the rival Catholic Church was hopelessly implicated in the perfidious sin of *traditio*—handing over the Scriptures. The body claiming to be free of this sin came to be called Donatists, after one of their early and notable bishops of Carthage. The first bishop of Carthage among the dissidents, Majorinus, was consecrated in 312 at a meeting of seventy bishops, hitherto Catholic, from the province of Numidia. The latter province was immediately to the west of Proconsular Africa whose capital was Carthage. Thus the dissident group began with a strong foothold in Numidia, where they were always to possess their greatest numerical strength. By the year 396, when Augustine became Catholic bishop of the Numidian coastal town of Hippo, there were more Donatists than Catholics in the African provinces. Something, obviously, about the Donatist Church held strong appeal for African Christians. This appeal was in large measure due to the tenacious preservation among the Donatists of traditions long cherished in Christian Africa.

Among the Donatists the memory and cult of the martyrs were maintained at white heat, a fact repeatedly brought to our attention from the early days following the persecution through the subsequent history of the movement in the next hundred years. It was a Donatist who edited the *Acta Saturnini*, a moving account of the martyrdom at Carthage of a man of that name and of his companions. Here we have all the familiar motifs of the peculiar glory of the martyr, of his fervid attachment to Christ, and of the special presence in the martyr of the Spirit of God. Here is also the stern warning, 'Whoever communicates with the traditors will not have a share with us in the kingdom of heaven',[1] words which in their precise form were doubtless placed in the mouths of the martyrs by the Donatist editor but which do not necessarily misrepresent the precise

sentiments of the martyrs in prison. At the close of the century
the Donatist bishop Petilian has in this regard made little
move to accommodate himself to the idea of a triumphant
Church militant. Christianity, he says, 'makes progress by the
deaths of its followers'.[2] Regard for martyrdom did not stop
at veneration for the victims who had died at the hands of the
state. One must, of course, distinguish between the views of
the Donatist leaders and the actions of Donatist folk anywhere
and everywhere. It is suggestive, however, of what one might
call the Donatist 'posture' that among their number were
agricultural labourers who seemed intent upon preserving a
likeness, a mirror, a caricature, of martyrdom, at a time when
the conditions of martyrdom were absent. We read of Donatists
who stopped travellers on the road and demanded to be killed
by them, and it was especially appropriate if the traveller
were a magistrate. We read also of a practice which makes
most sense if we see it as recalling the ministrations of the faithful to the martyrs in prison before their death: the friends of
a Donatist devotee gather at a predetermined place bringing
food, which the devotee then consumes before hurling himself
to a suicidal death in a river or in a fire.[3] Whether or not it
was expressed in such bizarre and pathological ways as this,
the Donatists were bound fast to the ideal of Christian martyrdom.

An African martyr whom the Donatists supremely honoured
was Cyprian. The Donatist literary remains which we possess
are pervaded by the language, the conceptions, and, to a very
appreciable degree, the spirit of the martyr bishop of Carthage.
From the *Acta Saturnini* through the argumentation of such
late Donatist writers as Petilian and Cresconius we repeatedly
meet explicit appeal to the writings of Cyprian, appeal to the
same scriptural texts as those to which he had appealed in
establishing the same or parallel points, and above all an
appeal to the authority of Cyprian for having separated
themselves from communion with Christians stained by the
guilt of *traditio*.

Briefly stated, the contentions of the Donatists were these:
the so-called Catholic Church in Africa, recognized as such
by the imperial and now 'Christian' government, has no claim
to that title; bishops of that Church at the time of the great

persecution handed over Scriptures to the imperial authorities and thereby committed an act which in the Christian Church is equal to the crime of idolatry; the guilt of this act, performed as it was by bishops, has spread as a contagion to all who have maintained communion with the churches of those bishops; there has been no alternative open to faithful Christians but to withdraw from communion with churches thus implicated; persons who seek membership in the true Catholic Church must be baptized in that Church, whether they come from paganism or from the profane sect of the *traditores*.

There was some measure of historical truth in the Donatist charges against the Catholic episcopate. Mensurius, bishop of Carthage, aided by his archdeacon and future successor Caecilian, had in fact resorted to a kind of subterfuge which recalls the old distinction between the lapsed proper and the *libellatici*: he had seen to it that certain 'heretical' books, probably Manichean, were handed over under the guise of their being Catholic Scriptures.[4] But it appears also that a number of the original Donatist bishops had themselves been *traditores*.[5] Some of the historical claims of the Donatists against the Catholic episcopate were probably fictitious and were asserted to be so by Augustine and by the courts of inquiry that had examined the matter earlier. There was on both sides ground for embarrassment over the historical point of the behaviour of the bishops during the great persecution. Neither side was inclined to face the damaging evidence pointing in its own direction, though, as we shall see, Augustine claimed that the historical point was in the last analysis irrelevant.

The importance of the Donatist case cannot be seen to lie in the validity of their historical claims concerning either their own or the Catholic episcopate. That importance lies rather in their shrill insistence that the African Church face honestly its own cherished traditions concerning the nature of the Christian Church in the light of the remembered events of the great persecution. It is at this point that Augustine is disappointingly opaque. Many words have been written by many people, from Augustine through a great company of scholars to this day, concerning the inconsistency of Donatist thought and Donatist action. But there is in fact a very remarkable degree of consistency attaching to their thought and

actions, given their initial premises and their fervid attachment to Cyprian. The question is to some degree that of what
one would mean by 'legitimate restatement', 'reformulation',
or 'development' in Christian thought and practice. The
Donatists did not live in static conditions any more than did
Augustine and the Catholics. They too were forced to make
decisions under the pressure of novel events. It sometimes
appears that Augustine, when he does not misunderstand their
point, wishes to require of the Donatists a kind of rigidity
and changelessness which he himself could not claim with respect either to the evolution of his own thought or to the
continuity of his thought with previous Latin Catholic theology.
Augustine put before the Latin world a theological structure
of breathtaking brilliance which did indeed possess strong lines
of continuity with previous thought but which was thoroughly
attuned to the new conditions of the Church in the empire. It
resonated with those new conditions much more than it did
with the conditions of a persecuted Church under a pagan
empire. The Donatists were sure that some important matters
had been forgotten. The particular lines of continuity with the
past which they chose, were different from those which Augustine chose, and they extended their lines in a different direction.

The Donatists operate from a Cyprianic understanding of
the unity and catholicity of the Church. To say that the Church
is Catholic means that it is a single, unique whole. One of the
chief marks of this wholeness is freedom from corruption,
freedom from stain. In its important and only decisive sense,
this freedom from corruption is the possession of the Church
if its bishops have not been guilty of infraction of that divine
law peculiarly placed upon them. The health of a body is
the health of its head; the stream flows from its fount; the stock
bears the mark of its 'origin', its root; and it is the bishop
who is the head, fount, origin, and root. A Church that is not
whole in this sense cannot be the Catholic Church. Bishops
guilty of the perfidy of handing over the Scriptures have in-
curred a stain of guilt such that they cannot approach the
altar of God to offer sacrifice, and they infect those with whom
they are in communion.[6]

To this degree the Donatists take with utter seriousness the
Cyprianic doctrine of the episcopate's relation to the Church.

If one reads between the lines, recalling the constant Donatist appeal to Cyprian, one conclusion seems fairly clear: to the Donatists it is apparent that bishops who were traditors in the great persecution have in that context performed an act of seriousness equal to that of pagan sacrifice itself or of securing a *libellus* from the authorities. The fact that the Donatists find themselves able to make this equivalence is one of the clear signs of the close association in their minds between idolatry and the imperial government. The Donatists did in fact bring charges that Catholic bishops had actually offered sacrifice as well.[7] It is to be remembered also that the act of 'handing over' issued in the burning of the Scriptures by government personnel who, officially, despised those writings. Such an act could not be taken lightly by people who treasured the written Law of God as revelation. Neither Augustine nor any Catholic writer was disposed to argue that *traditio* was a small matter.

Augustine's failure to take seriously the Cyprianic basis, the Cyprianic logic, of the Donatists can be illustrated from an incident in the earlier history of the movement which, Augustine thinks, provides him with opportunity to convict his opponents of self-contradiction. At a meeting in Carthage of 270 Donatist bishops, probably in the year 336, permission was given to the practice of admitting to membership those who came from Catholic churches without requiring that they be 'rebaptized', a decision which might appear to be out of accord with the Donatist claim that baptism in the church of the traditors is no baptism. The synod's action amounted to approval of a policy already practised, apparently, by a Mauretanian bishop Deuterius. After the synod's decision, we are told, the practice obtained for forty years among 'all the Mauretanian bishops'.[8]

To understand this decision we must recall that Cyprian had spoken of Novatianist schismatics and of idolatrous apostates in strikingly similar cultic language. They are both 'unclean', 'profane', 'adulterous'.[9] Both schismatic and lapsed bishops are under the same liabilities, regarding their holding of episcopal office, for reasons expressed in largely identical language. This would leave the way open, if one were so inclined, to put relations with schismatic churches on the same

F

basis as with a church whose bishops were traditors, *at least with respect to the admittance of laymen.* Cyprian himself had directed no less than three letters to Mauretanian bishops urging his position on the baptism of schismatics, and in two of these letters he declares finally his principle of non-interference in the affairs of bishops who do not baptize schismatics.[10]

If there is anything surprising at all in the action of the Donatist bishops in 336, it is that they in effect chose to treat individuals from the church of the traditors as having belonged to schismatic rather than apostate bodies, but for this they had ground in the writings of Cyprian. Augustine's paraphrase of his Donatist source leads us only to the conclusion that the bishops were willing to have Catholic lay people, *plebs*, received into the communion of the Donatist Church without Donatist baptism. The assembled bishops, therefore, can be seen as intending to extend to their colleagues from the province of Mauretania like episcopal privileges to those that Cyprian had acknowledged in letters to the same province. It appears that there was in Mauretania a long standing tradition of hesitance in insisting upon 'rebaptism'.

In the last decade of the fourth century the Donatists were embarrassed by the most distracting of the several schisms which troubled their history. A Donatist deacon of Carthage, Maximian, brought complaints of various sorts of inappropriate behaviour against his bishop Primian, and was successful in convincing the larger number of Donatist bishops in the province of Byzacena that he, Maximian, should be bishop of Carthage. Thus was inaugurated the Maximianist schism within Donatism, Maximian carrying portions of the more eastern provinces and Primian holding strong the allegiance of the West. At a council held in 394 the Primianists excommunicated Maximian as a 'dead man among the living' and in typical Cyprianic fashion warned him of the fate of being devoured in the earth as were those Old Testament schismatics, Dathan, Korah, and Abiram. The dissident bishops who had not actually joined in consecrating Maximian were given eight months to return to the Church without penalty. The consecrating bishops were damned as 'guilty of notorious crime'. Later, after efforts even of the secular power failed to drive two of the condemned bishops from their basilicas, the two were allowed to return as bishops to the main Donatist body bringing with them, without requirement of rebaptism, all whom they had baptized. The whole series of events provided Augustine and the Catholics generally with an obvious opportunity to observe that the Donatists were not serious in their claims either about the episcopate or about the sole validity of baptism within the one Church.[11]

Indeed, they were not strictly consistent. It is no part of our enterprise here either to defend the Donatists or to attribute to their actions a coherence which they do not possess. But the fact remains that the issue between the warring Donatist divisions and that between the Donatists and the Catholics were not quite the same. We observe among the Donatists in the 390s a momentum towards the preservation of their unity as the dominant Christian group in Africa. They maintain the old Cyprianic rhetoric against dissidents in their own ranks, but they know that the real confrontation is between themselves and the Catholics.

African Catholics themselves had responded to the pressure of the massive Donatist schism by closing their ranks with Catholics elsewhere, first on the issue of 'rebaptism'; there were, we can be sure, many African Catholics who swallowed hard when the Council of Arles in 314 required them to give up their ancient practice of the baptism of schismatics, and it was only a romantic imagination which allowed Augustine to think that the practice in question was of recent origin anyway.[12] Then the advance among Africans of the theory of papal primacy which we see taking place in Optatus of Milevis in the 360s and in Augustine is quite manifestly conditioned by the exigency of controversy with the Donatists.[13] The Catholics might be small in number in Africa, but they could rejoice in their unity with the apostolic see and with the whole Catholic world.

The Maximianist schism provided striking occasion for the Donatists to show by their action that they were not in fact totally bound by the Cyprianic past. It provided occasion also for them to demonstrate that in maintaining their own unity they could keep their attention fixed on their one religious and institutional *raison d'être*, which was to protest against Catholic acquiescence in the scandal of the great persecution. The Donatists in effect decided that in the context of the 390s, the Cyprianic call to separation and permanent deposition of schismatic bishops was less compelling than the same call in respect of lapsed bishops. Apostasy is more serious than schism. This is a judgement precisely the opposite to that which Augustine has reached in the year 401.[14]

It is not without interest that in 401–2 we discover the eminent Donatist layman, Cresconius, in a letter addressed to Augustine, stating how he thinks the Donatists ought properly to be regarded from a Catholic point of view. He is tired of the way in which Augustine in previous writings has freely spoken of Donatist 'heresy'. Heresy, he argues, means adherence to a different faith, whereas Donatists and Catholics share the same confession of Christ born, dead, and raised; the two parties have in common 'one religion' and 'the same sacraments'. The Donatists therefore are to be regarded not as heretics but as having created a schism.[15]

Cresconius' words here, and his comments which follow, suggest that a development has taken place in Donatist thought. The Donatists, we may speculate, in living through the turmoil of their own schism have taken a trick from Optatus and have learned to apply the distinction between heresy and schism, made originally by that Catholic author, to their own situation in such a way that they might justify their own shift in policy regarding 'rebaptism'. This justification, apart from the crucial distinction in terms, doubtless owes much to Augustine's many words against rebaptism. Augustine, in urging against the practice, had been given to pointing out that in many things the Donatists were at one with the Catholics, their only important errors being their remaining in separation and their practice of rebaptism.[16] It seems a likely hypothesis that the distinction between schism and heresy is developed by the Donatists under the pressure generated by their own Maximianist schism and as a way of putting their own theological house in order. Within two years the same distinction was to be used as a means of defending the Donatists against the imperial laws on heresy.

Cresconius sees that if one looks at one aspect of Augustine's position, it would appear that the difference between Catholics and Donatists is a difference simply between bodies divided by schism. But what Cresconius cannot understand is how Augustine, in calling the Donatists 'sacrilegious heretics', can seriously contend against rebaptism, because to call them this is to implicate them in the guilt of a 'nefarious and inexpiable crime'.[17] It is clear to Cresconius, following Cyprianic logic, that this other aspect of Augustine's polemic would seem to require rebaptism. One must be cleansed from such sacrilegious guilt before communion in the Church is thinkable.

And so Cresconius might wonder. His puzzle issues from the fact that though Augustine may give every appearance of doing honour to Cyprian, the legal and cultic force has been largely evacuated from this style of speech which Augustine has taken over from Cyprian. The two do not understand one another because both are appealing to Cyprian and because the Donatist alone preserves the Cyprianic meaning of the vocabulary common to them both.

Donatist puzzlement over Augustine's polemic was not confined to Cresconius. At the very opening of the letter which another contemporary of Augustine, the Donatist bishop Petilian, addressed to the Donatist clergy, he observes that while the Catholics find fault with the Donatists for their practice of rebaptism, the Catholics themselves by their baptism have stained their souls in a washing polluted with guilt.[18] It is important to see this observation as not simply an accusation against the Catholics but as a register of Petilian's confusion over the terms in which the debate has been conducted from the Catholic side. The Catholics are continually talking about rebaptism, whereas the prior issue is that of Catholic guilt proceeding from the traditors.

From Augustine's earliest letters concerned with the Donatist problem it is evident that from the beginning the practice of rebaptism was to him a profound source of outrage and of grief.[19] It is significant that the first period of his literary struggle with these opponents comes to a conclusion with the seven books *de Baptismo*, one of the longest of his many writings against them. Here we find ample ground for just the sort of confusion to which we saw Petilian giving expression above. Augustine appears to conduct much of the discussion on baptism as if they were not *Donatists* to whom he is addressing his remarks. Rather does the debate seem to be between Catholics who disagree as to whether schismatics ought to be baptized when they come to the Catholic Church. It is as if a fifth-century apologist for Stephen of Rome were arguing with Cyprian about correct Catholic policy, and as if the Donatists were in fact Catholics who had to be persuaded on Catholic grounds not to rebaptize schismatics. It is of course the case that Augustine addresses the work to a Catholic public. His discussion reveals the necessity to convince this public that it is neither necessary nor permissible to baptize Donatists when they come to Catholicism. This is the issue sometimes explicitly present but the hidden issue elsewhere present, and the fact that it is pervasive to such a degree offers evidence of continuing African Catholic opposition to the decision at the Council of Arles against the practice of rebaptism. But in the book *it is the Donatists who rebaptize*, and the case must therefore be directed against them. Is one to suppose that an important reason why Catholics went over to the Donatists was precisely the latter's continuance of the African practice of rebaptism; that Augustine in this work really has this problem in mind; and that his grief over the defection of Catholics for this reason, is in fact the ground of his repeatedly expressed horror of Donatist rebaptism? Probably.

In any case our point here could be formulated in the following way. It is one thing to offer, under Donatist pressure, a clarification of the grounds for Catholic refusal to rebaptize Donatists when they come to Catholicism. In doing this Augustine can be said in part to follow his announced intention in the treatise 'to refute the objections which the Donatists have been accustomed to make to us in this matter'.[20] It is another thing to attack the Donatists themselves head on and to attempt to refute them by appeal to their great authority Cyprian. Augustine tries to do both things in the work *de Baptismo*, and in the second he shoots wide of his mark. The Donatists could be excused their confusion in not being able to recognize themselves in a portrait in which their distinguishing features are deeply obscured.

Much of the argument of the books *de Baptismo* turns on the Donatist appeal to Cyprian. In the first book Augustine makes much of the point, to which he returns many times in many places, that Cyprian did not cut himself off from communion with bishops who did not follow his policy of rebaptism. In spite of his error on the matter of rebaptism, Cyprian's greatness lies in his devotion to the unity of the Spirit in the bond of peace, as opposed to the Donatists, who are conspicuously lacking in this devotion.[21] Augustine places the Donatist bishops in the position of having severed themselves, contrary to the example of Cyprian, from bishops who do not agree with them on the matter of the rebaptism of schismatics.[22] But the ground of Donatist separation from the Catholics is not that of such disagreement, and indeed we have seen above that the Donatists, following the example of Cyprian, were willing to tolerate in their midst bishops who did not rebaptize those who could be regarded as coming from a schismatic Church. The Cyprianic ground of Donatist separation is that the opponent Church descends from bishops who were traditors. Cyprian nowhere gives evidence of willingness to remain in communion with lapsed bishops and declares himself firmly to the contrary.

Augustine will carry this argument further and urge as follows: since Cyprian and his fellow African bishops did not sever communion with bishops who were of a different mind on rebaptism, the Church would have to have perished even in Cyprian's time on the Donatist theory of the contagion resulting from communion with 'wicked' men (the readmitted schismatics).[23] This argument overlooks the fact that the Donatist theory of contagion is thoroughly Cyprianic and depends entirely upon the peculiar role of the bishops in sustaining the Church's holiness. On this ground it is not the case, as Augustine seems to suppose, that pollution and destruction of the Church follow upon the presence of schismatic laymen who have not been rebaptized.

Augustine points out quite correctly that Cyprian acknowledged the presence of wheat and tares in the Church and reserved their separation for the coming judgement of God alone,[24] but neglects to notice that Cyprian used this language in respect either of laymen guilty of post-baptismal sin who were readmitted to full communicant status, or, at most, of clergy guilty of the same sin who were readmitted but whose status was evermore to be that of laymen. The Donatists were much too faithful to Cyprian to be over-concerned about the presence of sinful laymen in the Church.

Augustine comes closer to the point when he cites a passage from Cyprian's *de Lapsis*, in which the activities of marauding, greedy, fraudulent bishops are portrayed. He believes himself justified in supposing that Cyprian remained in communion with such bishops.[25] Perhaps, but three points may be put forward as relevant here.

1. In the passage in question Cyprian, writing just after the first wave of persecution has subsided, is painting a general picture of decadence and unfaithfulness in the Church prior to the outbreak of persecution and interprets the persecution as God's judgement upon the Church. It is not stated that Cyprian is dealing with a problem current and pressing at the time of writing.

2. So far as Cyprian in the work in question gives any advice as to the policy to be adopted in view of the many kinds of iniquity which he describes as having been committed by churchpeople, this advice is to flee from them because they spread contagion.[26]

3. The work *de Lapsis* was composed at a date before Cyprian had clearly worked out his precise position regarding bishops as the essential sustainers of the Church's holiness; here he regards all of the lapsed claiming readmission with *libelli* from the martyrs as spreading contagion,[27] a view which hardly corresponds to the picture of Cyprian which Augustine is eager to paint.

And so we could go on, but we shall not. Our intention in the above remarks has not been to sully the reputation of Augustine of Hippo. His achievement will outlast attacks from this quarter. The intention has rather been twofold: to illustrate the intensity of the crisis over the problem of the Church in Latin theology of the fourth and fifth centuries, and to illustrate how this crisis involved a bitter and wounding battle over the appeal to traditional authority. In the early years of the fourth century the Church had passed quickly from a situation in which leading and honoured bishops had been martyrs to one in which her leaders were the emperor's table guests and court advisers. The ambiguities attendant upon this transition, and the profound change required in traditional Latin eschatological thought relative to the empire, made necessary a whole new theological undertaking. The theology of Cyprian could not be pressed into immediate service for this enterprise on its own terms: that much the Donatists made unmistakably clear. On the other hand Augustine, whether or not he was aware precisely of the import of what he was doing, not only engaged in the required new undertaking, but in doing so freed the ongoing tradition of Latin theology from prominent aspects of the Cyprianic doctrine of the episcopate.

We turn now to a summary account of those aspects of Augustine's positive thought on the Church which most directly bear upon the ecclesiological controversy with the Donatists, and we leave to the next chapter the broader aspects, including the problem of the alliance of the Church with the state's coercive power.

Augustine returned to his native Africa from Italy as a layman in 388. In the year 396 he was bishop of Hippo and had already produced his first writings against the Donatists. It is important to recall two sorts of biographical data. First, African though he was, Augustine's powerful experience of conversion to Catholic Christianity had taken place at Milan; he had received his baptism at the hands of Ambrose, bishop of Milan; before he acquired intimate acquaintance with the Catholic churches of Africa, he had been a churchman already at Milan and at Rome; he came as a Catholic Christian to Africa. Second, his approach to the Church had been by way of a prior 'conversion' to Platonist philosophy; he had at Milan listened to catechetical instructions and sermons from Ambrose which were deeply coloured by that philosophy; he had become schooled to a synthesis of Platonism and Christianity by his own meditations, by his contact with Ambrose, and by his acquaintance with other Christian Platonists.

The importance of these considerations is not insignificant for our topic. Augustine's intense months as a Catholic in Italy were bound to make him look with the greatest scepticism upon a Church, large in Africa though it may have been, which virtually claimed that Catholic Christianity since the great persecution had been and was confined to the African

provinces. Through his encounter with Platonist philosophy
and by the windings of his own personal history he had come to
see the relation of a man, any man, with God in terms of a
pilgrimage, the pilgrimage of the soul towards final union with
God. The incorporeal soul of man is created to move towards
God, to thirst for him, to cleave to him, to love him. In contrast
to God who is immutable, the soul is essentially mutable,
which means that the soul in itself is morally unreliable. The
soul may be and is continually distracted from the course of
its pilgrimage by the impulses which come from its body,
by the objects of sense perception, and by its own wayward
motions. Though many setbacks may appear to interrupt
the soul's course, the soul that is on its way to God may know
that the divine illuminative power, working in hidden providential ways, will preserve it and finally lift it to its goal. It
belongs to the providence of God alone to know which souls
are thus begun and sustained in their pilgrimage, and why.

The soul does not walk its pilgrimage to God in a vacuum.
God in Christ is the creator of the soul and is the soul's inner,
hidden teacher, its source of light by which it knows everything
that it knows, and its source of goodness, by which it achieves
every moral conquest. But God in Christ is also the creator of
the whole world within which the soul is set, the world of
physical objects and of persons, other embodied souls. The
beings of this physical world possess their derived reality by
their 'participation' in, and their 'imitation' of, an eternal,
intelligible order of ideal forms, essences. This order of ideal
forms has its locus in the divine mind, the Word of God who
is Christ. The physical world is in a constant process of becoming, of progress towards and retreat from the ideal structures
of that intelligible order. However closely the beings of this
world approximate their ideal forms, this approximation
never moves beyond an approximation; the form achieved
in this world is always an imperfect realization of the ideal
form in that intelligible world; this imperfection attaches
also to the soul's own approximation of its eternal form.
Though Christ the Truth and the Light is always the soul's
immediate source of knowledge and of moral power, the
material order of God's creation—things, actions, words—
can and does perform the service to the soul of offering 'signs',

occasions in which the soul's attention is directed inward to the inner Teacher, to true knowledge, and to the source of moral goodness. God in Christ is the creator of the world which forms this kind of context for the soul's pilgrimage. But God in Christ is also the redeemer of the world who has come into its midst as the Incarnate Word and Son, who has been born, has died, and has been raised, and who restores men to love of himself in that society of love which is his body the Church.

Augustine's thought on the Church moves around two focuses: the Church is, on the one hand, a universal society whose purpose in the divine providence is to serve as the instrument by which God makes good his promises to claim men of every nation as his own; the Church is, on the other hand, a communion within whose bounds God, working through his appointed sacramental media and through the infusion of souls with the divine grace, draws men towards their final union with him in his future, heavenly kingdom. The Church is a universal society, and the Church is a communion of men animated by the divine Spirit, the divine grace.

It is a source of wonder and of scandal to Augustine that the Donatists can even entertain the notion that God after the great persecution had suddenly confined the geographical limits of his Church to the shores of Africa. Such a notion is both a denial of empirical fact and blasphemy. The Church had once played its role as a persecuted and tiny sect, and from those days the Church remembers with gladness the witness of many martyrs. But the facts have changed, and the facts as we now perceive them correspond precisely to the promise of Scripture that in the seed of Abraham all nations of the world would be blessed. Summoning his Donatist opponents to abandon their narrow preoccupations, he writes:

Let us not deal now with ancient documents, or public records, or minutes of civil or ecclesiastical courts. Our book is the larger one of the world; in it I read the fulfilment of the promise I find in the book of God: 'The Lord', it says, 'has said to me, "Thou art my son, this day have I begotten thee. Ask of me, and I will give thee the Gentiles for thy inheritance, and the utmost parts of the earth for thy possession"' (Ps. 2.7-8).[28]

To deny this coincidence of present fact with scriptural promise is to assert that God does not speak the truth; it is to take away from Christ the heritage that God has promised.

An integral part of the heritage foreseen in Scripture is the promise that not only the peoples but their rulers as well will come under the sway of Christ: 'All the kings of the earth shall adore him.'[29] Here was a crux in the mutual polemic of Catholics and Donatists. The Donatist failure to gain recognition from the emperor early in the fourth century ministered to their generally conservative theological position. Following on this failure they raised to prominence a motif not hard to find in Tertullian and not hard to assume in Cyprian: the rulers of this world have always been and always will be persecutors of the people of God. The Catholics have simply given further proof of their infidelity by aligning themselves with the ruling powers and by their complicity with those powers in coercive measures against the true Catholic Church.

Augustine's response is of the same dual form that we observed above. The present fact of the matter is that emperors are now in the Church, and this fact corresponds precisely to the scriptural promise that kings of the earth would serve Christ. It is necessary to be discriminating in the use of Scripture and to see that king Nebuchadnezzar, once a worshipper of idols and a persecutor, was then miraculously converted and issued laws on behalf of the true God. The situation of the pre-Constantinian Church is quite different from that of the post-Constantinian; one's view of kingship must change according to circumstances. The emperors of the post-Constantinian Church are called of God to be servants of Christ. Thus is Augustine confident that the Church is ordained in the providence of God to embrace the 'world' of the Roman empire and to absorb even that empire's rulers without diluting her essential character. The Church is a society dispersed far and wide and leading men of every rank of society to their true homeland in the heavenly kingdom to come.[30]

Augustine had in some way to come to terms with the tradition of African Catholic thought which formed part, an important part, of the background against which he thought and wrote. To envisage the Church in the way sketched above is immediately to raise the question of the Church's eschatological

purity and holiness. We can suspect from Augustine's view of
the relation of the soul to God that he would find it difficult
to integrate into his thought any notion of a purity or sinlessness
that would characterize either the Church generally or her
clergy. The suspicion is amply justified. We recall that Cyprian
had found use for Jesus' parable of the wheat and tares growing
together in the same field and had applied this parable to the
Church in a restricted sense. Augustine now picks up this motif
and makes it one of the major themes of his doctrine of the
Church. The Church as a whole is a 'mixed body'. The Lord's
parables of the wheat and tares, of the drag-net containing good
fish and bad fish, and of the sheep and goats—all apply directly
to the Church. Augustine was able to turn to fine effect against
the Donatists a dual appeal to both Cyprian and the letter
of Scripture. It was Cyprian himself who saw in the field of
wheat and tares a figure of the Church. But the Lord himself
in explaining the parable to his disciples stated explicitly that
'the field is the world'. So we have joined together on the
highest authority the two ideas: the Church is coextensive
with the world, and the Church has good and bad men in it.[31]

Augustine was too good a student of Scripture and had im-
bibed too much of traditional Christian thought not to know
that the Lord's parables and the idea of the purity of the Church
have an inherent eschatological direction. The wheat and
the tares stand together in the field until the reaping angels
do their work; Tertullian and Cyprian had been imbued
with the idea that men shall be now as they will be then. It is
precisely this eschatological reference that makes Augustine,
taking a cue from Cyprian, hold firmly to the growing together of wheat and tares now. It is only God who in the end
will separate wheat from tares and burn the tares in the fire
of his wrath. The Church's fishermen eagerly pull up the nets
teeming with good and bad fish, the Church sailing confidently
in the time left towards the end of the world as towards its
shore. The crucial mistake that the Donatists have made is to
confuse the end of the world with the time of Donatus.[32]

To leave the matter there, however, would be in effect
to give up the idea of holiness attaching to the Church as such.
Augustine does not abandon the idea but reconceives it and
redirects it along two lines, the first rather more dimly sketched

and the second much more clearly drawn. First, the Church is holy because of the holiness of Christ. Christ is the eternal Truth and Word of God, is himself salvation, sanctifying power. In him the Church as an empirical body can be said to 'participate', just as all the beings of this world possess their identity only through their 'participation' in their intelligible forms. The participation of the empirical Church in Christ may be an only imperfect realization of its true nature, but this imperfection the Church shares with all empirical entities relative to their archetypes. The Church is in no worse condition in this respect than anything else in the realm of empirical and historical reality. That which is unique about the Church among the things of this world is the uniqueness, the holiness, of that in which it peculiarly participates: Christ the eternal Word of God who has become man.

This is part of what it means to speak of the Church as the 'body of Christ': the Church is the earthly, empirical body which imperfectly imitates, participates, is 'joined to' Christ. Christ himself is unique among beings of the intelligible order in two ways: he is the eternal Word of the eternal God himself, and he has become incarnate in a man who alone conformed fully to the ideal of manhood. Thus, to speak of the Church's participation in Christ is immediately to speak of its conforming to the principle of manhood fully lived out in the life and death of Jesus. With all of the above suppositions in mind, it is right to say that the Church is Christ himself. The Church is the 'body' of which the eternal Christ is 'head'. 'The whole Christ is the head and the body'.[33]

The holiness of the Church is therefore grounded in the purity and goodness of Christ who alone gives the Church its identity.

But there is now a second way in which Augustine preserves the idea of the Church's holiness. This he accomplishes by giving to the word 'Church' two different applications, denotations. We shall see in the next chapter that the term has yet a third application. Here we are considering the term as it applies within this present, historical time. The word can denote the empirical, universal society with its ordained clergy, its sacraments, its celebrations—the total field of wheat and tares. It can denote also the smaller number of men within that society who are in truth being made holy by God—it can apply to the wheat alone. But the wheat, we may observe, is still growing and will continue to grow until it is 'reaped'. To speak more abstractly, there is no eschatological perfection in the historical Church, even on the narrower denotation of the term. The members of the Church within the Church must still be drawn towards their final perfection, must still be gradually released from their varying degrees of ignorance and infirmity, must continue daily to pray that their sins be forgiven. The Church that is truly and finally 'holy and without blemish', 'having neither spot nor wrinkle' (Eph. 5.27), is the Church which in the lives of these members is still 'being prepared'.[34] Thus the Church in its narrower but still historical sense may not be understood without reference to the Church in a third, heavenly sense, of which more later.

It is a primary thesis of Augustine that no man, not even a bishop, can rightly claim to distinguish here and now the wheat from the tares. One of the chief errors of the Donatists, he thought, was to attempt a premature separation of good from bad men. One must be willing to acknowledge the mysteriousness of the divine providence in leading individual personalities through long and circuitous routes. The thoroughgoing way in which Augustine has recast the problem of moral purity relative to the Church can be seen in his comments on the virtue of patience. We have noticed how for Tertullian and Cyprian this virtue is a mark of the Christian stance over against pagan society; in regard to that society one does not anticipate the avenging judgement of God, though for those writers the possibility of exclusion from the Church is always a real one. For Augustine the wrath of God will break equally upon the pagan world and upon many, perhaps most, in the Church. To attempt to uproot the tares from the Church is to be lacking in the virtue of patience, to refuse to allow to God what only he can do.[35] Augustine is simply following out the consequences of his close association of Church, world, and the 'field' in the parable of wheat and tares.

Patience does not mean the end of ecclesiastical discipline at the hands of the bishops. It means rather that the exercise of discipline requires much greater sensitivity and circumspection. The bishop still retains a magisterial function; he has at his disposal penitential remedies of varying degrees of rigor, and he may also excommunicate, if all other remedies fail. He exercises this office, however, not with any thought that thereby he must or can preserve an already achieved eschatological holiness for the last day; rather is his concern to maximize the conditions which will assist the faithful in their several journeys towards their final homeland. The weak brethren must be protected from influences leading them to fall; they must know that the wages of sin are serious; and the offending members themselves may be brought to amendment by the occasion of external 'persuasions'.[36]

It is necessary to emphasize the levelling effect which Augustine's conceptions have upon the problem of the Church's holiness. Cyprian saw clearly that the accepted penitential practice in the Church of his day and the critical events through which he lived, together made it impossible to posit the Church's holiness as a sinlessness attaching to the lives of Christian people generally. His solution was to posit the bishops as the bearers of a holiness which of course is in part 'moral', but which is understood in essentially legal and sacral language. The Donatists were largely faithful to Cyprianic thought. But Augustine will have none of it. The Lord foresaw that the Church would have evil bishops, and Christian hope is founded not on a man but on the Lord.[37] The Cyprianic view requires that a man receive the Holy Spirit from a man who possesses it, that a man be baptized at the hands of one who is without guilt, that a man be given his faith by one who has not had his faith made null by contracting a contagious infection. In the Donatist view contagion radiates from the 'origin', 'the root' of the Church which is located squarely in the episcopate.[38] Augustine will not acknowledge the Cyprianic origin of this idea and claims misleadingly that Cyprian taught the impossibility of communicated guilt in the Church.[39]

The effect of Augustine's teaching is to moralize and to individualize the category of 'holiness', and to place the whole matter within the context of the journey of the soul towards God. The Christ who came once and who is to come again is now also a sustaining, dynamic principle of movement and of growth, a transcendent presence who is related to his people by innumerable lines reaching to the inner lives of those whom he is drawing to himself. Augustine, bishop of Hippo, can say with the fullest equanimity and with the most confident faith that even if it had been proved that he himself was a traditor, he would feel not the slightest necessity to leave the Church, 'where I am able to be changed for the better'.[40] Though Augustine's language continues to have much legal vocabulary in it, this vocabulary is softened and made more religiously useful by its being taken up into a new conception of the relation between Christ and his people.

If we turn to the problem of the unity of the Church, much that was said above concerning its holiness is directly relevant. The Church is one in the most fundamental sense because of its union with the transcendent Christ as his body. This unity is not a 'unicity' in the sense predominant in Cyprian. It is a unity that is present through a far reaching multiplicity and multiformity—differing penitential practices, differing levels of progress in sanctity, differing degrees of knowledge of God and of theological insight. This unity in multiplicity has its most revealing expression in the spirit of charity, of love, which binds Christians together in peace and in concord. This spirit is in fact the Holy Spirit of God, who is the living principle of the Church's existence. Where the Spirit is present, there is the 'love of unity'. Love, most basically the pressing thirst of the soul for God, includes in its scope a determination of the will to preserve the peace and concord of the Church. Those who sever themselves from unity and erect a schismatic Church have proven that they do not live by the Spirit of charity and are not in the Church.[41]

But the question may now suggest itself, Are there no clearer marks, signs, by which one can recognize that Church which is animated by the Spirit of God? Augustine's attention to transcendent ideals and to peace and concord did not take his attention away from the form of the Church as an empirical society. Just as in the case of holiness, so in the case of the Church's unity and identity, the language of law and of the Church's 'constitution' is clearly present and indeed is indispensable for Augustine. There are marks which indeed identify the Church as that empirical society which is the body of Christ, and the living together in mutual relations of charity and communion is not the only one of these. The Church of Christ is the Church which holds to the Scriptures and which

G

confesses one Trinitarian faith. It is, moreover, the *Catholic* Church. Argument over the meaning of the word 'Catholic' recurs throughout the literature of the Donatist controversy. The Donatist contention, as we saw, was that the term connoted a special kind of wholeness, and that that Church can be called 'Catholic' which is obedient to the whole of the divine law. Catholicity was for them defined in terms of the holiness and integrity of the Church and of her sacraments.[42] Augustine insists that the meaning of this problematic word is given in that coincidence of the promise of God with present fact of which we spoke above. That is the Catholic Church which has a universal geographical extension, as opposed to the sectional, schismatic, African Church of the Donatists.[43] The term, there-fore, for him, has a meaning much conditioned by the necessities of controversy, and in fact in adopting this meaning, Augustine follows his predecessor in anti-Donatist polemic, Optatus of Milevis.[44]

However, closely related to the idea of Catholicity under-stood in this sense, is the consideration that the African Catho-lics, as opposed to the Donatists, are in relations of peace and communion with those widespread churches which were founded by Apostles and whose succession lists are open to inspection. Chiefly but not solely important in this regard is the Church of Rome. The bishop of Rome enjoys a priority of honour among all bishops of the Church, and Augustine himself at the end of his life is not intolerant even of juris-dictional appeal to that bishop when a mess has been made of things among the Africans.[45]

Augustine's wide ranging and scarcely systematized thought leads us to say that in the situation of controversy within which he wrote all of these external signs of the Church are present and simply support and reinforce each other: Scrip-tures, creed, universal extension, and the communion enjoyed among and with the churches of apostolic foundation. Together these form the visible 'shape' of the one Catholic Church.

But we have left out an important element in the Church's visibility: the sacraments. We have seen above that the Church's unity can be defined either with respect to its transcendent ground and inner spirit, or with respect to its external marks. Both of these are held firmly together, and it would be misleading to say that the one or the other is more dispensable. We described the Church's holiness in terms of its transcendent ground and the quality of life to which a number within the larger Church are drawn. Within this schematism the sacraments can now be seen as the visible marks of the Church's holiness. Augustine's importance for Latin sacramental thought is to be seen in his clear distinction between the sacraments as objective 'signs' and the question of the worthiness of those who participate in them either as ministers or as laity. The Donatists raised the problem in a special way with their claim that a sacrament cannot perform its proper role in the relation between God and man unless the officiating minister is, in their sense, pure. To Augustine the Platonist it seemed nonsense to suppose that the way in which God can use a 'sign' of his grace is in any way dependent upon the moral quality of a minister or of those in whose company one receives. There is, we might say, a triangular scheme set in motion, or many triangular schemes, when a sacrament is celebrated: God, the faithful who receive, and the objective sign which God employs as the occasion of the working of his grace. The essential features of a sacrament are its external, sensuous nature (its *species*), and its being accompanied by words of the Gospel. A sacrament is 'divine', holy; by it God 'brings about spiritually a man's consecration to himself'.[46] To be sure, the inner disposition of faith is necessary in order that sacraments be effectual unto salvation, but that is not the point here, which is rather that the sacraments possess the character of being objective signs through which God sanctifies his people. They are instruments of the divine providence, and as such their operation is entirely independent of the character of those administering them.

We have seen that for Augustine the Catholic Church is that society whose principle of life is the Holy Spirit of God, the Holy Spirit of charity, and that to depart from this Church in schism is to deny charity and to lose the Spirit. The Donatist controversy forced Augustine to bring the above sacramental teaching into relation to his thought on the unity of the Church. In the background of course was the dispute between Cyprian and Stephen over schismatic baptism, as well as the conciliar decision at Arles requiring the African Catholics to desist from their practice of rebaptism. The sacramental dispute between the Donatists and the Catholics centred largely on the question of baptism, and to the Catholic Augustine the question posed itself as to the significance of Donatist baptism, given the fact that they are not rebaptized when they come to Catholicism. Here Augustine adopted a formulation by which he intended to hold both to the objective sanctity of the divinely appointed sacrament and to his doctrine of the Church.

Though the sacrament of baptism, and in fact all the sacraments, are sacraments of the Catholic Church and have their home, their proper locus, there, the Donatists can no more defile or obliterate these sacraments than they can injure either the one God or the one Christian faith which they confess. There is 'one Lord, one faith, one baptism' (Eph. 4.5). But neither the one God, the one faith, nor the one baptism is of any use to the Donatists. Baptism is not of avail unto salvation for those who have departed from the unity of the Church and who are without the Spirit of charity. A soldier who has once received his branding in the imperial army retains that external sign even when he is a deserter; it is not given to him again when he returns. In upholding the sanctity and objective character of the divinely appointed sacrament Augustine has seen fit paradoxically to argue that the sacrament can be truly present when only the external sign is there. Augustine the Platonist lives in a world of signs which either are or are not perceived as signifying their true realities, depending upon the inner disposition of the soul; this Augustine has come to the service of Augustine the Catholic churchman who finds himself pressed by hard circumstance to reconcile Stephen of Rome with Cyprian of Carthage. The Donatist receives true sacraments of God but is prevented from enjoying the vivifying effect of those sacraments by the fact that in his wilful separation from God's Church he arrogantly excludes himself from the life of the Spirit of God, the Spirit of love, who vivifies the Church. Stephen, Augustine suggests, did not know how to defend that correct policy which he had received from ancient custom.[47]

The correlation of a proper attitude of soul with the effectual working of the divine Spirit is central to Augustine's anti-

Donatist ecclesiology. But he applies the same correlation to those within the Catholic Church as well, a fact which qualifies his Catholic exclusivism with a certain hard-headed realism. The Catholic Church is the place, the only place, where the Spirit of God is at work.[48] Within that Church are many who participate in the sacraments but who are not 'spiritual' men, who are false deceivers and depraved, whether publicly or inwardly; of them it must be said that they do not receive the sacraments to their profit any more than do hardened Donatists.[49] The Catholic hardened in his hypocrisy and the schismatic hardened in his schism are, in the only sense that really matters, equidistant from salvation. Both receive valid sacraments, both to no avail. Both of them are 'outside' the Church understood as the 'body of the one uncorrupt, holy, chaste dove, which has neither spot nor wrinkle';[50] the schismatic is simply outside more visibly, more openly.[51]

Augustine was indeed thinking about something else as he listened to the Donatists. He was, we may suspect, preoccupied with the creative struggle to state an essentially new Latin doctrine of the Church.

4

AUGUSTINE:
THE CHURCH OF THE ELECT AND
THE TWO CITIES

The bulk of Augustine's anti-Donatist writings had been completed by 411, the year in which took place under imperial auspices the protracted conference at Carthage between bishops of the opposing churches. The conference ended in a decision by the presiding officer, Count Marcellinus, against the claim of the Donatists to be the Catholic Church of Africa. Marcellinus ordered that Donatist communities be disbanded and that their property be confiscated, an order reinforced by edict from the emperor in the following year. These events brought the long controversy virtually to an end, though it appears from the correspondence of Pope Gregory the Great that there were still Donatists in Africa almost two centuries after the Conference of Carthage. Augustine thereafter devoted a large measure of his remaining literary activity through some nineteen years to two projects, the combating of the Pelagians and the writing of his imposing apologetic work, *The City of God*.

Both Augustine's anti-Pelagian thought and *The City of God* possess direct relevance to the subject of the Church, a consideration of some importance to us here. The heart of the Donatist controversy had been precisely the nature of the Church. A recurring topic in the anti-Manichean treatises had been the 'authority' of the Church, the persuasive weight of an institution rich in tradition and deep in civic esteem, an 'authority' which Augustine sets against the Manichean claim that their religion is founded on reason. It is not the case that the Church is a subject peripheral to Augustine's interests. It might have been the case that had he remained a layman and lived in monastic retirement enjoying the company of congenial intellects, he would not have applied his mind to precisely those issues which his career and sense of responsibility as a bishop in fact thrust upon him. But as events transpired, his attention was drawn to that very subject, the Church, which had long been and was long to remain a central concern of Western theology. It is only a contemporary bias which might maintain that his heart was not really in it.

As is well known, the issues in the Pelagian controversy which came to the surface as the predominating ones were those of the nature of man as both creature of God and sinner, the meaning of human freedom, the nature of divine grace, the relationship between grace and freedom, and the significance of human sexuality, the latter subject arising from Augustine's teaching on the manner in which original sin is transmitted. These subjects are in themselves beyond the scope of our attention here. It is essential to point out, however, that accompanying these great issues and in part underlying them is the old question of the purity or holiness of the Church. The British monk Pelagius is to be seen not so much as introducing theological novelty into the Western Church of the early fifth century but rather as reintroducing into that context an archaic view of the holiness properly attaching to the Church.

Pelagius was no less persuaded than was Augustine that apart from the grace of Christ men are bound by the power of sin. The difference between them on this subject was over the origin and nature of this power. To Pelagius it is to be entirely explained as the power of social conditioning and of habitual action. To Augustine it is to be explained as the power of a human nature vitiated in the person of Adam the first man who can pass to his posterity nothing more than that vitiated nature which he has come to possess. It cannot be doubted that these contrasting views are pregnant with consequences for the respective theologies of the two men. But to the question, Are men now able to be without sin apart from Christ?, the answer of both is clearly no. This leads to the further point that for man *as we know man*, which is surely the religious issue of central consequence, redemption in Christ is of equally crucial importance for the two figures. The view cannot be maintained that God or Christ, or both together, are peripheral to the theology of Pelagius.

The central religious difference between Pelagius and Augus-

tine, if one may be allowed the distinction between religion and
theology, has to do with the character of the Christian life and
therefore with the character of the Church. To Pelagius the
life of the Christian is a life aided by the indispensable example
and teaching of Christ, and spurred on both by the hope of
heavenly reward and by the fear of divine judgement. This life
is one of obedience to divine commandments, commandments
of a God who is just and who therefore could not conceivably
command the impossible. Any view less stringent than this
and which excused man's failings as due to a fault of his nature
Pelagius condemned, too simply, as partaking of that Manichean heresy which saw sin as inescapably inherent in man's
bodily, fleshly, nature. To 'Manichean' teaching of this sort
Pelagius returned an answer similar in form to the standard
response of second- and third-century Christians over against
numerous forms of Hellenistic fatalism, viz., a man is free to
obey the commandments of God who is just and who is the
creator of heaven and earth, including man's nature.[1]

The freedom of the Christian to obey the commandments of
God implies for Pelagius the possibility that he be without sin,
since sin is any action contrary to a divine commandment.
But this is equivalent to saying both that we are commanded
to be without sin and that we are able to be without sin.
Pelagius' perfectionist doctrine of the Church is of a piece with
these theses. He finds it the most natural thing in the world to
convert his language concerning the 'righteousness' of the
Christian and the 'ability to live without sin' into language
concerning the holiness of the Church. A scriptural text which
he repeatedly recalls is Eph. 5.27, in which the Apostle Paul
speaks of the Church as 'without spot or wrinkle or any such
thing . . . holy and without blemish'.[2] Those who are stained
with sin are not in the Church.[3] In the structure of that holy
temple which is the Church it is impossible that there be stones
which are not holy.[4] 'It is assuredly we who are the Church
though on condition that we live, as commanded, without
fault and stain.'[5] The important Pelagian concept of the Church
as the body of Christ, emphasized at many points in Pelagius'
commentary on the Pauline epistles,[6] is not at all to be understood in anything approaching an Augustinian sense; the
Church as body of Christ conforms itself *fully and by definition*

to the divine will for man, which means that its members obey the commandments of God.

Pelagius' sense of the Church as being Christ himself in his members corresponds with surprising closeness to the perfectionist doctrine of Tertullian. Though Tertullian does not characteristically speak of the Church as the body of Christ, he shows no hesitation in saying that the Church is Christ himself.[7] Pelagius and Tertullian, then, share a perfectionist view of the Church which can be expressed in terms of the identity of Christ and the Church. Now that this extent of common ground has been uncovered, it will be instructive to note briefly some further points of similarity between them: a decidedly legal way of defining the character of the Christian life, with obedience to divine commandment as a prominent motif; a threatening, pervasive, expectation of the violent cataclysms and terrible revenge of the divine judgement coupled to the complementary expectation of blessed rewards for those who persevere; a confident belief that life in the eschatological kingdom is a *real* (and not simply anticipated or partial) possession of the Christian in the midst of this life;[8] a grounding of the possibility of full obedience to God in human freedom as against 'necessity' or fatalism under any name;[9] a heavy investment, so to speak, in the sacrament of baptism as the moment in which the new life is opened out to the Christian— all of these striking likenesses are present in addition to other more minute matters which this is not the place to investigate. Our point in making these observations is not so much to assert a direct literary dependence of Pelagius upon Tertullian, though it seems not unlikely that the later writer had some acquaintance with the earlier. Rather the point is to illustrate, by reference to the subject of an earlier chapter, the fundamental continuity of Pelagius' thought with an earlier kind of Western Christian piety, reaching back into the second and third centuries. There is much truth in the thesis, at least so far as the patristic period is concerned, that heresy is basically conservative, or rather archaizing, whereas Catholic writers tend to move forward into new situations with new modes of theologizing.

In the degree to which the Pelagian controversy was a controversy about the nature of the Church, Augustine had already confronted a similar though not identical problem in his controversy with the Donatists. To simplify matters a bit, though not, I think, basically to distort, one could say that the Donatists presented to Augustine an archaic theology of the Cyprianic type, whereas Pelagius presented an archaic theology of a Tertullianic type. There is at least this much truth in such a thesis: the Donatists held a perfectionist doctrine of the Church in which the Church's holiness devolves upon her bishops; Pelagius held a perfectionist doctrine in which there is no peculiar necessity laid upon the bishop as preserver in his person of the Church's holiness, but rather in which all baptized persons are either within or without the Church according as they have sinned or not sinned after their baptism. It must immediately be said that at a number of points the parallel between Pelagius and Tertullian breaks down, as can be seen from the absence of the distinction in Pelagius of lighter sins and sins 'against God', and from his willingness to allow to the bishops an authority to modify the Church's disciplinary practice.[10] The old way of conceiving the effect of sin upon membership in the Church does not in the end work very well for one who can look with equanimity upon adjustments in disciplinary practice and who must admit when pressed that he himself is not without sin.[11] One encounters in Pelagius the bizarre spectre of individuals now in the Church and now out, their re-entry, in some cases at least, being conditional upon their performance of penance.[12] Pelagius will speak of sin as neglect of the commandments of God and will be at pains often to emphasize the binding obligation of all God's commandments upon men, even those which might appear 'lighter' and of less consequence than others.[13] Infractions of even 'lighter' commandments are sins. Reading between the lines, one seems to see in Pelagius a reaction against the distinction between lesser and weightier sins on the ground that this distinction has become occasion for a virtual disregard of all but those sins which require the rigour of 'second repentance'. Pelagius wants to make with the greatest urgency the important religious point that all sin is 'contempt of God' and to be avoided.[14] This is significant, for it displays that Pelagius, while in the very course of advancing one of his most moralistic theses, is straining away from a conception of sin as simply 'act'[15] and is attempting to state a somewhat different conception of sin as an orientation of mind or of soul. In Pelagius this attempt amounts only to an occasional and suggestive groping.

All of these considerations add up to a perfectionist doctrine of the Church that is showing signs of stress, not to say breaking down. An essential part of the older perfectionism had been the distinction between degrees of sin, and it is this distinction that Pelagius is unwilling to make.

It will have become apparent that in his anti-Donatist writings Augustine had already laid down the basic lines of his reply to Pelagian perfectionism. Life without sin is understood not primarily as freedom from particular acts, transgressions of divine commandments, but as that freedom which consists in the soul's unified and spontaneous love of God, the cleaving of the soul to God as its only true good. Such a freedom is not to be expected in full degree while the soul is in pilgrimage this side of death. In the earlier writings against the Pelagians Augustine chooses not to be intransigent and simply announces his inclination to believe that no man except Jesus Christ has been without sin.[16] By the year before his death he had turned this inclination into a dogmatic proposition; the thesis that no one in this life is without sins of some kind is one of three principal points which the Catholic Church has to make against the Pelagians.[17] It is of significance to note that Augustine makes this point precisely in reference to the Pelagian teaching that the Church is 'without spot or wrinkle'.

It is clear that the Pelagian controversy did possess direct relevance to the doctrine of the Church and that in fact this issue was one of the deeper ones at stake. In the previous chapter Augustine's doctrine of the Church in relation to the problem of sin was discussed more fully than is necessary here. This doctrine is in the Pelagian controversy powerfully combined and reinforced by the set of conclusions which Augustine had reached in an exegetical work written shortly after his elevation to the episcopate and addressed to his old acquaintance Simplician, now bishop of Milan: the Apostle Paul means to teach that the salvation of men is accomplished wholly by the electing will of God, whose grace so moves men's wills that they are turned to have faith in him, love him, and delight to obey him in their 'advancement' towards himself.[18] Augustine's developing polemic against the Pelagians is compounded essentially of these two ingredients. Now the problem of the Church's holiness is related directly and explicitly to the conversion and sustaining of human wills by the power of divine grace. The saints, now holy by conversion and baptism but not without sin, move towards their final sinlessness sustained by the divine grace. The observation may not be out of place here that the Augustinian concept of the Church is more adequate than Pelagius' teaching in resolving the tensions and contradictions manifest in Pelagius' own writings and utterances. A recasting of the doctrine of the Church's holiness was an urgent item of the theological agenda at the turn of the fifth century, and Pelagius himself, in the midst of his insistent effort towards moral reform, unwittingly bears testimony to this urgency.

There is a second direction in which the Pelagian controversy affected the problem of the Church in Augustine's thought; here again we must refer to an essential aspect of his anti-Donatist thought. Augustine, we recall, can employ the term 'Church' either to denote the visible Catholic Church with its ministry and sacraments or to denote the smaller company, within the larger body, whose hearts are truly aflame with love of God and who are being drawn to their heavenly destiny. Such a twofold conception of the Church is an inevitably ambiguous one, the question arising, at least implicitly, as to the positive significance and necessity of the sacraments. Augustine's answer to this question had centred in a conception of the sacraments as holy and divinely instituted signs which either are or are not received to the 'profit' of the participants according as they are rightly disposed in affection and mind. The net effect, it must be said, of the Pelagian controversy on this issue is to disrupt the equilibrium of the two senses of 'Church' in Augustine's thought and correspondingly to weaken the significance of sacraments as signs and instruments of the divine grace.

Augustine sees the relation of the future heavenly kingdom to both the individual and the Church here and now as the relation of a final destiny to those progressing slowly towards it. Once this relation is seen clearly and unambiguously in these terms, and once the philosophical problem of the relation of the soul to the divine is defined and solved in a conception of will transformed and moved by the empowering divine grace, Augustine finds it natural and in fact necessary to formulate a new theological conception of freedom. The raw material for such a new formulation lay close at hand in the old Roman conception of *libertas*: the freedom of the citizen to enjoy and to participate in the civic life of the commonwealth, a conception that was closely linked both to the notion that such freedom operates within circumscribed limits of law, morality, and religion, and to the notion of security from danger. Freedom for Augustine then is no mere autonomous power of choice between alternatives. It is rather the freedom of a man who is already a citizen of the heavenly kingdom and city of God, who enjoys the chief good of that city in his love of God, whose ultimate destiny is not in danger, and who when he finally reaches that destiny will be indefectibly protected even from the danger of any form or shape of sin.[19] This freedom is nothing but gift of God. The word for the divine activity in grasping, moving, and sustaining the will of man is 'grace'. Thus has Augustine worked three transformations: of Roman *libertas*, of the ancient Christian affirmation that redemption in Christ brings to man freedom, and of the equally ancient Christian belief that the kingdom of heaven is open to men by the gratuitous favour of God.

This manner of relating the gratuitous activity of God to a conception of men's laborious pilgrimage or progress to a heavenly destiny represents an impressive achievement in the thought of Augustine. But he was forced to further clarifications in the face of somewhat friendly but highly critical questioning from monastics, first in Africa and then in Gaul. The group of monastic theologians in southern Gaul who are usually (though misleadingly) called 'semi-Pelagians' were nothing but pleased at Augustine's conception of entirely unmerited and sustaining grace as they measured this conception against the general position of the original Pelagians. But the Gallic theologians were ascetics deeply informed by the example and writings of Eastern fathers who had written with eloquent introspective power of the struggles, setbacks, and conquests of the soul as it battles temptations from without and within on its way to final purification and union with God. The Gallic monastics were quite sure that Augustine's doctrine of grace unfailing in the working of its purpose detracted from the reality and the

significance of the soul's struggles, nor was it able to give satis-
factory account of the painful contrast between those who fall
away from the Christian life and those who persevere. And that
first crucial moment in the soul's relation to God, the moment
of turning to God in faith—it too must be an act of autonomous
choice, they thought, though God could be said to prepare the
human heart for this turning and in this sense to anticipate
every human movement towards himself.

Augustine was no stranger to introspection and was no
enemy of ascetic monasticism; he, too, at the end of a long
career as a sensitive and highly observant bishop, had long had
cause to ponder the defection of Christians from the life of
faith after apparently the most promising beginnings. Augustine
was not in the habit of shielding himself from the force of
empirical fact, and the fact of Christian defection was one of the
brute data garnered from his experience in the episcopate. But
such a fact did not at all exert its force in the direction of
weakening his fundamental conviction of the utter dependence
of man upon God. Rather, the facts prompted Augustine to a
deepened wonder at the mysteriousness of divine providence[20]
and to a further explicit modification of the notion of the Church
of the saints.

God's ways are past finding out. They are in fact so far past
finding out that Augustine is moved to take account of problems
worrying the monastics in the following surprising way: God's
redemptive grace, though it offers the only security possible to
men, does not securely lead all men whom it touches to the
completion of their redemption; some do not receive the gift
of perseverance. It is the case, according to Augustine, that
God does regenerate some in Christ; does give them faith, hope,
and love; does call them, justify them, and renew them in
baptism (all of these being gifts of grace); yet does not give them
perseverance.[21] They may be called, but they are not 'called
according to the purpose' of God and are not among the predestinate.[22] But this means that they are not in the Church, on
the narrower denotation of that term, because the Church in
this sense is the fixed number of the predestinate.[23]

Augustine might not have been amused by the very words in
which we have put his point. But it is not easy to be sympathetic
to his way of putting his point. The difficulty, at least from a

logical point of view, is that Augustine is not quite consistent enough in pursuing his theme of the total dependence of man's will upon God. God, he maintains, is responsible for all the Godward movement of man's will, both for the initial gift of faith and for the indispensable *gift* of perseverance. Yet when it becomes necessary, in face of hard fact, to notice and account for the defection of the faithful in argument with the monastics, Augustine adopts the device of holding men responsible for falling away from grace. '. . . They receive the grace of God, but they last only for a time, and *they do not persevere*; they forsake and are forsaken; for they are sent away in accord with their free choice by the righteous and hidden judgement of God, *not having received the gift of perseverance.*'24 The African monks who read Augustine's work *de Correptione et Gratia* may well have rejoiced to read the words, 'And they do not persevere', and may have thought that that was enough, not quite understanding the rest. But one can grasp why the more sophisticated and persistent critics of Gaul thought that the end of the matter had not quite been reached. The clauses quoted above cannot be defended by appeal to the paradoxical and ambiguous character of Christian existence. They are simply confused.

What Augustine has done is to place the faithful (all of whom have received regenerative grace) in a position, relative to the grace of perseverance, precisely parallel to that of fallen man relative to regenerative grace as such. In both cases God acts completely without respect to human merit in infusing grace into some but not others. The race of fallen men, having never been touched by grace, sin by their own free choice in the sense that to sin is what they want to do. A like 'free choice' of sin is now attributed to the regenerate in Christ who do not persevere. This means nothing else than that the redemptive grace of God is from one point of view sometimes defectible, that it sometimes does not effect the proper work of grace, which is to recreate man, convert his will, and return him to his proper orientation as lover of God.25 But that the divine grace sometimes fails in these ends is one of the very points which the critics of Gaul are at pains to urge, only they wish to say that this happens because the free wills of men fail to co-operate. Augustine, as we have seen, is willing to say much the same thing. His position is that the redemptive grace of

Christ converts the wills of all the regenerate so that they become lovers of God, that some of these by their free choice do not persevere, that perseverance is entirely a gift of grace distributed by the hidden judgement of God, and that perseverance is the kind of gift which in the nature of the case cannot be refused.

There is a deeper reason than a purely logical one for suggesting that there is unresolved confusion in Augustine's mind. He works with more than one model in attempting to rationalize the problems of perseverance and defection. The contrast between the regenerate who receive the gift of perseverance and those who do not is on the one hand parallel to the contrast between those of Adam's fallen race who receive the grace of Christ and those who do not.[26] But Augustine appears to see the regenerate who do not persevere also on the model provided by Adam before his fall. Adam received that grace which would have enabled him to remain without sin but which by free will he could forsake. This grace given to the first Adam is to be sharply contrasted to that grace which is 'in the second Adam'; the former would have enabled Adam to live in righteousness if he had so willed, while the latter brings it about that men in fact will to live in rightousness. Adam 'forsook and was forsaken', which is the precise language Augustine uses in speaking of the regenerate who do not persevere.[27] In one frame of mind, therefore, when considering those who do not persevere, Augustine seems to see redemptive grace 'in the second Adam' as if it were like that grace which the first Adam could and in fact did forsake. The confusion resulting from the blending of these two models is close to the heart of the difficulties in Augustine's late anti-Pelagian treatises.

The effect of these considerations upon the doctrine of the Church is to make the inner, essential Church increasingly into a theological postulate and to make its relation to the empirical Church more tenuous than had been the case when Augustine was disputing with the Donatists. The distinction between the two senses of 'Church' had been a move against the confidence of the Donatists that it is possible here and now to work an empirical division between the holy Church and those who by their lapse defile the Church and in fact destroy it if they are not identified and expelled. While asserting the impossibility of such an empirical division because of the hiddenness of sin in the soul, Augustine had none the less emphasized repeatedly that the Church in the narrower sense is to be distinguished in principle from those not belonging to it by the quality of life of those who are indeed aflame with the love of God, and he had made this emphasis even when already in the anti-Donatist writings he was saying that this Church is the company of the predestinate.[28]

The basic change in this regard is signalled by the relative absence of reference in the earlier writings to the scriptural text, Romans 11.33, and the continual reference to it in the writings of the Pelagian controversy.[29] 'O the depth of the riches and wisdom and knowledge of God! How unsearchable are his judgements and how inscrutable his ways!'[30] Augustine had called the text to his service early in the controversy for the support of his conviction that the redeeming grace of Christ selects some members of Adam's fallen race, quite irrespective of their merits, and converts them while passing others by. The same text appears for the same purpose in the last phase of his anti-Pelagian writing but now for another purpose as well: to offer scriptural support for the thesis that the gift of perseverance is bestowed upon some who have been blessed by the grace of Christ but not upon others.

In the writings of the Donatist controversy the Church which is truly the pure bride of Christ is to be identified with those within the empirical Church who bring forth the fruits of faith in both outward act and inward disposition, plus those whom the grace of God has not yet placed within this company but will so place before they die. In the later writings of the Pelagian controversy Augustine has drawn a yet smaller circle within this one. The essential Church is to be identified as those now within the empirical Church who both show the fruits of faith and are predestinated to receive the gift of perseverance, plus those whom God will place in this company before they die. Augustine, incidentally, nowhere shows ground for supposing that after the historical appearance of Christ any will be among the predestinate who have not been baptized before their death, and in many places gives evidence that he regards baptism in this life as a necessary condition for gaining the kingdom of heaven.[31]

H

These considerations mean that any human attempt now to accomplish an even provisional delineation of the boundaries of the essential Church relative to the empirical Church is in principle even more impossible than had been the case along the lines laid out in the Donatist controversy. Participation in Catholic sacraments, a life currently informed by faith, hope, and charity, a heart aflame with love of God—not one of these nor all of them together allows a man to suppose that he is in the 'Church' in the only sense that ultimately matters. The Frankish theologians of the ninth century who reacted so violently to the revival of Augustinian predestinarianism at the hands of the monk Gottschalk were not wrong in supposing that one of the issues most centrally at stake is whether it can be the case that by eternal judgement and decree, participation of faithful men in the Church's sacraments be futile and delusory.

It has not been our intention above to offer a complete account of Augustine's controversy with Pelagians and 'semi-Pelagians' but to sketch the main ecclesiological components of this controversy. Let us summarize our conclusion to this point.

To the Pelagians' perfectionist theory of the Church's holiness Augustine responded with a conception of that holiness whose basic elements had already been formulated in controversy with the Donatists. This conception is now combined with a new conception of the 'freedom' proper to citizens of the heavenly kingdom. It is combined also with a conception of grace which reflects Augustine's sense of the total dependence of men upon the unmerited favour of God. The doctrine of grace is correlative with an understanding of the character of Christian life as laborious pilgrimage towards a heavenly destiny, the arrival at which will for the first time bring fully sinless perfection to the lives of God's elect saints. Augustine's monastic critics, themselves taking with utmost seriousness the very notion of a progress towards perfection that is essential to Augustine's own thought, raise the questions of the reality and seriousness of moral struggle and of the human contribution towards victory. Augustine responds in such a way as to draw a parallel between on the one hand Christians who persevere relative to those who do not, and on the other the regenerate relative to the unregenerate; as in the one case, so in the other, grace is unmerited gift.

Augustine's account of the issue of perseverance means that to some the regenerating grace of God is not given to the end that they may be finally delivered to the heavenly kingdom of God, but for some other purpose. Augustine professes not to see very far into this mystery, but to the extent that he can see, he draws again upon the parallel just stated: God accomplishes in this awesome way a demonstration of the impossibility of any security in this life except as his unqualified gift, and thus teaches regenerate men not to be 'high-minded';[32] so severely unsearchable are the divine judgements and so palpably clear must it be that salvation is of God alone, that God will choose one man for perseverance over another in spite of their both possessing roughly equal degrees of that 'merit' which itself has consisted in nothing but grace-given faith and good works.[33] Thus is brought to a harsh finale the development of those themes from the anti-Donatist writings and from the books to Simplician which had from the beginning supplied Augustine with the stuff of his anti-Pelagian polemic. The essential Church of the saints and man's dependence upon unmerited grace— when the combination of those two conceptions is challenged by the monastic question concerning perseverance, Augustine gives his answer in terms of the Church of the predestinate whose members are elected by the unsearchable judgement of God to receive the gift of perseverance.

It is not without significance that an important section of one of Augustine's final anti-Pelagian writings should be devoted to the subject of the Church holy and without blemish.[34] Here it becomes clear that his final teaching may be viewed as an answer to the question, 'Would God choose the unholy and the unclean for membership in that Church?' Augustine must be equally as emphatic as a Pelagian or perfectionist of any stripe in returning a negative answer to that question; he shares this much ground with the eschatological perfectionism of both his own day and of previous Christian centuries. The effort to return this negative answer became in his case an effort to say no both to that and to a further question: 'Is the holiness of God's people their own achievement, either now in the time of their perseverance or in the future heavenly kingdom?'

It seems appropriate to add some brief reflection on Augustine's method of stating and supporting his final position on

perseverance and predestination. It has been suggested above
that this final position, at least from the point of view of the
regenerate who may not be among the predestinate, goes some
way towards weakening the positive significance of participation in the Church's sacraments by faithful people. There is a
curious irony to be observed in the way in which Augustine
supports a doctrine having this tendency by an argument
drawn from the Church's practice of infant baptism. At issue
here is a further aspect of that parallel already noted between
the predestinate and those who are initially made regenerate at
baptism. In the course of the Pelagian controversy Augustine
made use of arguments concerning infant baptism in relation
to both of these parallel issues. Commentators on Augustine
have long noticed the fact that early in the controversy he
supported his doctrine of the presence of original sin in infants
by appeal to the practice of infant baptism: the Church baptizes
infants (for good and sufficient reasons, he thinks); baptism,
by tradition coming from Scripture, is 'for the remission of sins';
in some sense, therefore, sin must attach to infants.[35] In this
context he had gone on to sound the theme of the inscrutable
judgement of God which brings it about that of two infants,
both equally 'sinners' and equally deserving of the divine wrath,
one is given access to the kingdom of God by baptism and the
other not; or that of two baptized infants, death takes one away
while he is still innocent of actual sins, while the other survives
and becomes a wicked man.[36]

In the later writings Augustine revives this line of thought,
both turning it to a new purpose and bringing it to a conclusion.
He turns it to a new purpose by repeatedly stating it as a key
model for the understanding of the wondrousness of divine
election in giving perseverance to some while hardening others;
God's pattern of election is constant in both infant baptism
and in the giving of perseverance.[37] He brings it to a conclusion
by explicitly drawing under the sway of providence the man
who is baptized in infancy and grows up into wickedness.
Whereas before, it was said that this man in infancy is simply
'going to be' a wicked man, now it is said that he is destined
by eternal judgement to be hardened in heart.[38] Not for nothing
has it sometimes been suggested that Augustine, arguing in
such a vein from the sacramental practice of the Church,

indulges in a method of theologizing which, perhaps in an unfriendly spirit, might be labelled 'ecclesiastical positivism'. To be more friendly, one might observe that Augustine is here simply applying to this particular matter a method of theological argumentation not at all rare in patristic authors, viz., argument from the practice of Christian worship. The proper evaluation of this method remains one of the more urgent and provocative problems of contemporary theological scholarship.

In the course of drawing attention to the baptismal model which he proposes in support of his doctrine of perseverance, Augustine allows us to see the core of the problem as he perceives it. The holiness of the saints in this life is a holiness that is always distant from its final purity. This conception of a gradual and not always forward 'progress' Augustine had to state not only in the face of heretical perfectionism of his time but within an entire ecclesiastical setting in which the institution of 'second repentance' still held sway, with its attendant concentration upon particular kinds and acts of sin, whether grave or otherwise. Augustine cannot say often enough that the saints have continually to pray that their sins be forgiven. That saints are sinners is a problem, not a platitude. This means that from his point of view it is not implausible to look upon faithful, regenerate *sinners* in the same light as that in which he looks upon the whole 'lump of perdition' which is the unregenerate mass of humanity.[39] Regenerate sinners possess merit indeed, but it is a merit that is entirely the work of divine grace. Grace itself, however, is an aspect of the working of that general divine providence which has presided over the fall of man in Adam and over the whole history of unregenerate man. With respect to what men of themselves have achieved in positive movement towards God, both unregenerate and regenerate stand precisely equal. The sins of the regenerate, Augustine must say, are to be laid at the door of these sinners themselves, as is the case with the sins of the unregenerate; they both sin by free choice. The conclusion is fairly evident to him: the regenerate have no claim upon the mercy of God and may justly be condemned for their own sins, which means that God may justly withhold from them the gift of perseverance.[40] In this way we may grasp the structure of the problem as it presented itself to Augustine. He made a bold attempt, not always carefully considered, to face the realities of life in the Catholic Church of the Roman empire, to continue to affirm that the Church is holy, and to express his conviction, rooted in personal experience and informed by the reading of Scripture, that man's happiness is due entirely to the unmerited grace of God.

Thought about the Church assumes broader proportions when we turn to *The City of God*. Augustine's great apologetic work is a difficult book, easy to get lost in and easy to seize upon in its particulars for one-sided tendentious interpretations of its author's thought. A balanced, historical, full-scale analysis of the whole is sorely needed today and obviously cannot be attempted here. But a few introductory comments are essential if we are going to see even one aspect of the work in its proper perspective.

Interpreters of *The City of God* are often inclined to analyses that are too simple. On the one hand they point to the sack of Rome by the army of Alaric the Goth in 410 and contend that Augustine directed his work against pagan charges that this event, causing a tremour of shock throughout the Western empire, was what could be expected once Rome had forsaken her ancient gods. This line of analysis has two distinct points in its favour. First, it has the authority of Augustine himself.[41] Second, it helps to account for much of the content of the work. For otherwise Augustine would surely not have devoted such detailed attention through five books to argument concerning the relation between pagan worship and the temporal vicissitudes of the Roman state since its founding. The question, 'Where were your gods then?', is one which resounds throughout the first five books as Augustine catalogues one Roman defeat after another in the attempt to prove that the gods had never reliably insured military victory.[42] This line of interpretation also goes far in illuminating much that Augustine asserts and implies regarding the relation between Christianity and the temporal prosperity of the Christian Roman Empire and of every earthly city, as Lloyd Patterson has recently pointed out. Once Augustine diverts his primary attention from the history and idolatrous religion of Rome and begins his exposition in Book XI of the origins of the earthly and heavenly cities, two of his leading motifs through twelve books are the pride and lust for domination which govern every earthly city as such, and the distinct ends, aims, of the heavenly and earthly cities. Implicit wherever these themes appear is the conclusion that must be drawn concerning the relation between Christianity and the Roman empire whose official religion is now Christian: it should never have been thought that the Christian worship of the true God would preserve Rome from an event which was, after all, 'occasioned by the customary procedures of war'.[43]

There are, on the other hand, aspects of the work which remain puzzling when the above view has been given its due: the learned digressions into pagan Latin literature and the details of pagan worship; the pedantic expositions of material from the Roman antiquarian Varro; the frequent and notable fastidiousness of style; and the remarkable volume of words devoted to the views of the neo-Platonist philosopher Porphyry. The reader who comes for the first time to Book xxii, thinking he has been encouraged by the author to expect an imaginative and serene scenario of 'the eternal blessedness of the City of God', is disconcerted to find Augustine continuing his unrelenting argument against particular points in the pagan critique of Christian belief, prominent among which are the views of Porphyry and the Platonists on the impossibility of a bodily resurrection.[44] *The City of God* comes from the pen of a man who is in control of the literary and philosophical culture of the Roman world and who does not mind displaying to his readers just how firm and far reaching that control is. His first and immediate public was a circle of pagan Roman intellectuals who had begun to appear on the north African coast in flight from the terrors of Alaric in Italy. Such men would have doted on the *Saturnalia* of Macrobius, a work whose author was a Platonizing and erudite antiquarian and which presented, with loving and fastidious detail, reflections and lore drawn from Roman literature and religion—all in the form of a symposium whose participants are distinguished Roman pagans of the closing decades of the fourth century. This second line of analysis, then, sees Augustine as a once pagan and now Christian intellectual; in *The City of God* he comes to terms with that part of his own life moulded by a 'classical' education; he gives an account of himself to a circle of Roman conservatives whose interests run to the antique, who are trying hard to hold up the old tradition, and who themselves can be sincerely religious

men, their piety and thought deeply informed by the great
Platonist philosophers.

Each of these two lines of analysis goes awry roughly to the
degree that it tries to edge the other out of sight. It should be
seen that the conservative intellectuals to whom *The City of God*
is immediately addressed are not without interest in the political
and military fortunes of the Roman empire; the empire itself,
needless to say, would form the indispensable setting for the
revival of everything they hold dear. Part of their traditional
way of life had been participation in public affairs; one of their
heroes was the senator Symmachus, memorable for his pleading
in the 380s with the Catholic emperor that the altar of Victory
be allowed to remain in the senate-house. Augustine himself
accuses these very people (who should know better, having a
'taste for history') of having deliberately encouraged the spread
among the uneducated masses of the charge that the recent
disasters are due to Christianity.[45]

Augustine is not ignorant of the reign, fifty years back, of
Julian the apostate emperor, a man who surrounded himself
with Platonist intellectuals and whom Augustine implausibly
ranks beside Nero and Herod as a persecutor of Christians.[46]
From the time of his own adult life Augustine recalls two other
figures who had appeared on the horizon as possible leaders of
a return to paganism: the Gothic chieftain Radagasius, whose
expedition into Italy up to the environs of Rome in 405–6
had encouraged pagans of the capital to predict (erroneously)
his victory through the aid of the gods to whom he performed
daily sacrifice; and Eugenius, the Roman professor of rhetoric
turned usurper, who in 394 had attempted to lead a pagan
revival but had been happily quashed by the Catholic emperor
Theodosius I. Indeed Augustine makes special point, amidst his
surprisingly lengthy remarks on Theodosius, of commenting
that that emperor, when faced with unfavourable military odds,
had not given himself over (like Julian) to 'wicked and forbidden superstitions' but had sought the prophetic voice of a
Christian hermit in Egypt, and, assured of victory, went off to
achieve it.[47] Augustine does indeed view the empire with a
certain cool detachment as not in principle different from any
other earthly kingdom founded upon the 'lust for domination'.[48]
Yet he is not indifferent to the status of Christianity as the

religion officially sponsored by the empire for the worship of the true God; he approves Theodosius' legislation against worship of idols,[49] and, of course, had defended imperial repression of the Donatists.

Augustine tells us at the end of the fifth book of *The City of God* that 'certain persons' had already written a rebuttal of the first three books, the theme of which books had been the unreliability of the old gods in protecting Rome from military defeat. These persons had not published their rebuttal but were waiting for a time when they could do so 'without danger'.[50] What would such a time be except one in which paganism would not be actively proscribed?

The years of writing *The City of God* are years of mounting uncertainty in the West both for the old empire and for the fortunes of the Catholic Church within that empire. The anxiety is discernible in Augustine's recurring words on the 'adversities' of the Church.[51] The sack of Rome had provoked a vigorous pagan reaction in the ancient capital. Not Italy alone was at stake; in 406 Gothic tribes crossed the Rhine into Gaul and quickly spread as far as the south of Spain, a vantage point from which they were within twenty years to launch a successful campaign to conquer Roman Africa. Gaul was distracted by invading tribes and by usurpers of the throne. Britain became detached from the empire. This left Africa as the one remaining imperial stronghold. But Africa was not immune to shocks occurring elsewhere. The panic attendant there upon the Gothic ravages in Italy had led the authorities in Carthage to a temporary suspension of the laws against heresy; indeed an essential aspect of the renewed suppression of Donatism after 410 was the attempt to preserve a unified Africa as the one place where the Catholic Western Empire still possessed its integrity. In Africa danger lay not only with Donatists at home and Vandals in Spain. There came to be increasing numbers of Gothic-Arian mercenaries among the imperial troops stationed there, accompanied by Roman officials showing a tendency to dally with Arianism;[52] and to the south the nomadic tribes were rising in active rebellion which the military commander of Africa was disconcertingly slow to quash.[53]

The conclusion suggested by these considerations is that Augustine in the thirteen years of writing *The City of God* has good cause to sense these years as times of fearful confusion whose outcome is not at all clear. Certainly one possible outcome is a renewed and widespread revival of paganism. He wants, therefore, to offer every available argument against the pretensions of idolatrous religion. He wants also to define the relation properly to be discerned between Christianity and the well being of the Roman empire or of any earthly kingdom that might embrace Christianity. In regard to these issues his programme is, in short, to argue three points:

1. Neither pagan nor Christian religion insures a state against the temporal and military vicissitudes common to states as such.

2. As regards religion, the Roman empire can do nothing better than to be a Catholic Christian empire and thereby further among men the worship of the true God.

3. The ultimate destiny of Catholic Christianity is not in the slightest degree tied to the fortunes of the Roman empire.

In doing these things he addresses himself to cultured men of antiquarian interests whose minds are deeply informed by Platonist thought. They are men with whom Augustine shares a heavy debt to Platonism as well as to a whole Latin cultural heritage, and they are the very sort of men who could play an active role in any revival of paganism. It would therefore be much too simple to say that *The City of God* is a book about the sack of Rome. But the sack of Rome offered more than simply an occasion prompting Augustine to a full exposition of a theme long present in his mind and writings. The fall of the Western capital was such an occasion, but bound to it were issues of central importance to the content of *The City of God* itself.

Looking upon *The City of God* from the perspective adopted in this chapter and the previous one, we may see in it a third prolonged literary effort against archaism, in this case the archaism of paganism fortified by Platonist philosophy. Included in this archaism is a view of the relation between religion and the commonwealth which sees religion as the guarantor of the commonwealth's temporal prosperity and military hegemony. This view had not only pagan proponents. A Christian version of it had appeared early in the fourth century in the writings of

Eusebius of Caesarea. Modern authors have sometimes been tempted to suppose that Augustine advanced his views on the relations between the two cities, earthly and heavenly, in conscious antithesis to Eusebius. The most tenable position on the question of Augustine's knowledge of Greek Christian writings is still that he gained such knowledge as he had almost entirely through Latin translations. This means that of Eusebius Augustine will have read little beyond Rufinus of Aquileia's translation and continuation of the *Ecclesiastical History*, in which of course Rufinus does, on the Eusebian model, write about Theodosius in virtually messianic terms. The 'imperial theology' here in question, however, was not peculiar to Greek and Eastern writers. Besides Rufinus it had in the West found eloquent spokesmen in the poet Prudentius and in Ambrose of Milan. It may in fact be that one reason for Augustine's rather puzzling reticence concerning the eminent bishop whose preaching had played an important role in the months before his conversion and at whose hands he had been baptized, is Ambrose's espousal of a view concerning the relation between Christianity and the empire with which Augustine came to be increasingly out of sympathy in the decades following his years at Milan. Quite apart from whatever theoretical demurrers one might have wanted to advance in an atmosphere of calm reflection, the imperial theology common to Eusebius and Ambrose was no longer plausible in the Latin West, once the Gothic tribes had started their march.

It is intriguing how Augustine in *The City of God* develops lines of thought which both contribute to the apologetic direction of the work and at the same time are centrally relevant to issues not immediately apologetic in character. This feature of the work makes it Augustine's most comprehensive and systematic statement of his total theological position. As we turn our attention now to matters more narrowly concerned with the Church, we may discern this feature immediately in his treatment of the subject of angels.

The Church begins with the angels before the creation of man and his world.[54] Augustine in his younger days had been once so attuned to the Platonist doctrine of the heavenly homeland of the soul that he had found it possible to write of the soul 'returning, as it were, to the realm of its own divine

origin'.[55] He had rather quickly moved away from such a thought
and by the time of writing Book XI of *The City of God* takes
occasion to criticize that venturesome Christian Platonist,
Origen, for having taught that the souls of men descend into
bodies as the result of having sinned by abandoning God; the
doctrine impugns the goodness of God's material creation.[56]
This digression on Origen occurs significantly in a book of
which the leading subject is the creation of the angels and their
subsequent division by reason of the fall of some of them. The
doctrine of the heavenly Church of the angels serves as Augustine's substitute for Origen's scheme. It is not the case that the
souls of men first existed in heaven, are now embodied, and are
summoned to return to their place of origin. But it is the case
that spiritual, non-material beings are the first citizens of that
heavenly city which is the homeland of the elect saints here;
the angels have 'invited us to their society and have desired us
to be their fellow-citizens there';[57] we shall one day be 'equal
to the angels' and are now angels 'by hope';[58] 'we and they
together are one city of God', we on pilgrimage here, and they
lending us their aid from above.[59] The doctrine of the pilgrimage of the saints towards their homeland of angelic beings
existing before the creation of man and his world is the nearest
the mature Augustine can approach to the Platonist teaching of
the return of the soul to its homeland. Once the significance of
angels relative to man is thus established, a clear alternative is
posited to the pagan practice of offering sacrificial worship to
angelic beings, a practice which serves as a main target of
polemic in Book X; the writings of the Platonist philosophers
themselves bear witness to the one true God, yet that eminent
Platonist Porphyry inconsistently encourages superstitious worship of beings who truly will only that men join them in their
worship of God.

There is a closer link which Augustine establishes between the
Church here and the society of the unfallen angels. A place
has been prepared for the elect before ever man was created.
The gap left in the angelic company by the fall of Satan and his
hosts is to be filled up by the company of predestinate men.[60]
By this move Augustine nicely fits into a total doctrine of providence the problem, so baffling to men here, of predestination
and perseverance, and by the same move he brings into even

closer alignment an original creation of super-terrestrial beings with men destined to enter the society of such beings. Augustine allows us to see by a telling comment the basic correlation in his thought between the angels and the nature and destiny of men: '. . . I have undertaken to speak of the origin of the holy city and have thought fit to speak first of the holy angels, who not only form a large part of it but are all the more blessed because they have never lived in exile.'[61]

The problem of the identity and stability of the Church of the elect, raised acutely in the latter phase of the Pelagian controversy, finds in Augustine's teaching about the angels some clarification by being placed in a broader, more cosmic scope. The City of God has, first of all, a permanent membership in the angels who did not fall and who have been endowed with grace such that they will never fall.[62] This is the Church which endures 'immortal in the heavens', and whose members know with unfailing certainty that they will abide always in their enjoyment of God.[63] These angels *persevere*.[64] Augustine finds thus in the division between fallen and unfallen angels a third model for understanding the contrast between men who persevere and men who fall from grace. Holy men and holy angels are so closely correlated that to the angels, too, does the Pauline text apply, so repeatedly cited in the anti-Pelagian writings, 'The love of God is poured forth in them by the Holy Spirit bestowed upon them.'[65] The doctrine of grace becomes in Augustine so entirely an aspect of the general providence of God that angels who never have and never will require redemption in Christ are seen to require the very grace so urgently commended by the Apostle Paul. Another way to put the point would be to say that dependence upon the grace of Christ's redemption is the particular form of dependence upon God appropriate to fallen men.

Concerning the contrast between fallen and unfallen angels Augustine allows himself to be more consistent than when arguing with his monastic critics on the subject of perseverance. Either it is the case that the fallen angels at their creation receive a lesser amount of the 'grace of the divine love' than did those who persevered, and therefore they fell; or it is the case that all the angels are created equally good, and the persevering angels are then 'assisted more fully' than those who fall by their evil will.[66] Augustine leaves both these alternatives open, saying nothing as to which is to be preferred. Even if one opts for the second, and leaves the fallen angels to fall by their 'evil will', two points are worthy of note: 1. The persevering angels are said explicitly to be 'assisted more fully' than the others; 2. The falling angels have no previous sins to their debit and so cannot be said to be punished in receiving less grace than the others. Augustine has here reached a bald and honest statement of the matter, a statement in which two of his fundamental theses are clearly displayed: the electing grace of God discriminates among rational creatures without basis in any merit that might attach to them, and the will of men to cleave to the good is wholly dependent upon the sustaining divine grace. Without the divine grace the will of the rational creature becomes a bad will.

It is perhaps not surprising that Augustine had not allowed himself to be so open in disputing with Christian monastics who championed a conception of 'free choice' quite different from his. To pagan Platonists this statement of the matter would have seemed clearly and naturally of a piece with the aesthetic account of the problem given some chapters earlier in *The City of God*. God creates men and angels whose future wickedness he foreknows will be contrasted to the goodness of others, 'thus embellishing the succession of the ages as if it were an exquisite poem enhanced by what might be called antitheses'. Just as in a poem the contrast of opposites lends beauty of language, so is the beauty of the course of this world built up by a kind of 'rhetoric of things'.[67] It needs only to be added that in the teaching of Augustine God's foreknowing disposition of the created order is nothing different from predestination.[68]

The effect of *The City of God*, then, upon problems concerning the Church arising out of the later anti-Pelagian writings, is twofold: to set the pilgrim Church of the predestinate within a wider and cosmic context as the number of those who will replace the fallen angels, the number of those who will enter fully into the blessedness of a Church existing eternal in the heavens; and to expose the meaning of grace in its relation to perseverance by supplying a model which in its simplicity and clarity does not suffer from the contradictions attendant upon the blending of the two models previously noted.

Anyone who writes about the Church in *The City of God* must be expected to say something about the relation of the Church to society. The point must first be made that the whole work is about this subject, a point which must be taken with complete seriousness. In speaking of the City of God Augustine is speaking of the Church. Modern readers have been conditioned by interpreters from a number of schools of thought and theological traditions to make various fine distinctions in Augustine's language—Church, City of God, Kingdom of Heaven, Kingdom of God, Body of Christ, and the like. Most such distinctions simply will not hold. It is not the case that Augustine uses 'Kingdom of Heaven' to refer only to the future heavenly society or to the company of the predestinate here. 'Kingdom of Heaven' can denote the present empirical Church with its mixture of good and evil men, some of whom are among the predestinate and some not.[69] 'Church', 'holy city', and 'City of God' can refer, all in the same context, to the predestinate,[70] while 'City of God' can elsewhere denote simply the empirical Church, including some within who are 'bound to her by the sacraments', but 'who will not be with her to share eternally in the lot of the saints'.[71] It would be tiresome and inappropriate in this context to argue and document the point further. Scholars have been much too eager to adapt Augustine to their own theological sensibilities. The fact of the matter is that he can use any one of a number of terms equally to refer to the unfallen angels, the empirical Catholic Church, predestinate men, or predestinate men plus the unfallen angels. It is on the other hand not quite to the point to accuse him of being loose and vague in his use of these terms. He was much too conscious of a weighty theological tradition behind him not to apply 'Church' with all of its surrogates to the visible Catholic Church with its sacraments and ministry, and he was much too much a Catholic theologian to be disposed towards diverting any of the terms applying to the people of God away from that visible structure which he believed to be an essential instrument of the divine providence; and he was much too convinced, also, of the surprises which that providence could work to attempt any premature sorting out of those who might be said to belong only to the 'visible Church' as opposed to those belonging to the heavenly kingdom. But he knew that within the 'Church' were many who were not truly called of God. The conceptual framework within which he can be seen to have viewed this problem and to have written with reasonable consistency, was suggested in the previous chapter. Once the reader has discerned the various possibilities within Augustine's language, it is usually not difficult to discover his meaning.

It remains here only to remark on the significance of Augustine's naming the crowning work of his life *The City of God.* With equal accuracy relative to his own meaning it could have carried the name 'Church of God'. But the work was apologetic in its direction. It is natural, therefore, that he should have adopted a term which places the Church in immediate relation to the political commonwealth whose destiny recent events in the Western empire had made a matter of urgent concern. In so naming and conceiving the work, moreover, he drew upon the theme of the 'two cities' that had been present in his writings since the year 390.[72] The import of this fact lies in our seeing that Augustine did not first begin to think about the relation between Church and society after the sack of Rome. If that had been true, he could have produced only a superficial tract for the times. The apparent crisis of the Western empire gave direction and form to a project and theme on which he had long cogitated.

The political commonwealth, in popular opinion, is in danger. The real danger has to do both with a proper understanding of the relation between the true religion and the commonwealth's prosperity, and with the future of that religion in the Roman commonwealth. The theme of the commonwealth has been a recurring one in the philosophers, reaching back, through Cicero, to Plato's *Republic.* The Christian Scriptures speak of a city of God: 'Glorious things of thee are spoken, O City of God.'[73] So Augustine writes a work about The City of God which is his *magnum opus* and which in being that is yet further evidence of the centrality of the Church in Latin theology.

In speaking of the relation between Church and society Augustine pursues with fair consistency a method which has properly been called a method of 'juxtaposition'. This device represents Augustine's adaptation, for methodological purposes, of a principle which we have discovered to be prominent in the thought of both Tertullian and Cyprian: the Church is an alternative to the idolatrous society of the Roman empire. Living now within the imperial Church, of whose status Augustine is far from disapproving, he has now to adapt the principle. His adaptation may be summarized as follows: the Church is an alternative to that society of fallen men whose principle of association is the pride and lust for domination giving rise to the Roman empire and to every earthly 'city'.

The most basic antithesis of all is that between two 'loves', which have formed two 'cities', societies. Augustine lays bare this antithesis by a combination, essentially, of two moves. He takes his cue as to the nature of a 'people' from the Church itself and from the bond which is the inner principle of the Church's identity—love, love of God in the case of the Church; that which fundamentally unites any 'people', then, is love of some kind; to this degree Augustine operates with a theological model of the nature of the state. His second move is to consider a classic definition of a 'people' found in Cicero's dialogue, *de Re Publica*: a people is an 'assemblage united in fellowship by a common sense of right and a community of interest'.[74] The meaning of Cicero's definition was never fulfilled in the Roman republic, Augustine argues, because according to Cicero there can be no republic without justice, and the most important kind of 'justice' is lacking where men do not give the true God his due and where they descend to the degrading worship of idols. So Augustine revises Cicero's definition to read, 'A people is an assemblage of rational beings united in fellowship by their agreement as to the objects of their love.'[75] The Roman state, the Greek, the Assyrian, and all other individual states are themselves member provinces of a single 'earthly city' united by love of self and lust of domination. Over against the earthly is the heavenly city, the Church, formed by love of God and humble contempt of self.[76] The contrast between earthly and heavenly cities here has in its background the contrast between fallen and unfallen angels; the two cities began not here below but there above. God is king of the one city and the devil of the other.[77]

It is impossible, I think, to mitigate the severity of this contrast in Augustine's thought, given the historical context within which he wrote. To write about the kingdoms of this world was for him to write about the concrete reality of a gigantic empire

I

within which he lived and which he saw in a line with other
expansive empires of which he had some historical knowledge.
Lust of rule has existed among the Romans in more unmitigated
intensity than among any other people. The empire of Augustus
brought a reduction of civil liberties. The prospect of Rome's
possible success in making her boundaries coextensive with the
whole world and in thus establishing a kind and degree of peace
is not really very promising, since the very extent of empire so
far attained has produced social strife and civil war even more
obnoxious than wars of imperial expansion.[78] Of course it
belongs to the divine providence to turn the wrath of man to
divine purposes. God has been pleased to use Rome as the
instrument of bringing peoples far and wide under a unified
sway of laws.[79] Some ancient Romans possessed notable virtues
prompting them to personal sacrifice for the good of the commonwealth, but this good was precisely an earthly good, and
those Romans have had their reward.[80] It is true that we do
find Augustine looking with favour upon a scheme of small
states that might have lived in peace with one another and
rejoiced 'in neighbourly concord'.[81] But this possibility he
regards as a lost one. We do not find him much interested in
theorizing about an ideal political scheme which unfallen man
might have enjoyed. Augustine is not a political theorist. He
gives an account in theological language of the concrete
realities of political life structured by fallen men.

Even if the Romans can be said on occasion to have waged
'just wars' against small neighbour states, they none the less
waged such wars with the desire, universal in the earthly city,
to subdue and govern those whom they fought. The formation
of large empires is the concomitant of this universal desire. The
Roman empire is thus the supreme exemplification of the
structure of existence inevitably characterizing the earthly city.
The contrast between the earthly and the heavenly cities is a
stark one, based upon a contrast of loves, and having as its
present visible manifestation the juxtaposition of Church and
empire.

To this root contrast attach a multiplicity of others. Here we
may see Augustine following in the footsteps of his Latin predecessors, though with notably less interest and emphasis
upon the structural and legal aspects of the Church as an in-

stitution. Once the fundamental contrast has been stated as a
contrast of loves, Augustine is less concerned than his fore-
runners to make the City of God into an image of the City of
Man. Tertullian and Cyprian had seen the Church locked in
combat with a persecuting, idolatrous empire; they had fought
to elicit the loyalties of men to a community that in principle
offered at every point a parallel to their lives as idolatrous
Romans. Augustine is far from abandoning this outlook. Christ
is 'King and Founder' of the City of God.[82] The Church in its
ministry and laity has its own 'governors' and 'subjects' who
serve one another in love, the latter by obeying, the former by
giving counsel.[83] To the heavenly City belongs a 'true liberty
freeing its citizens from the dominion of sin and a 'glory' which
will be theirs when the suffering of this present time have been
cast off.[84] In contrast to the quasi-scriptural authority of
Virgil stands the 'teaching of divine Scripture', 'the store of
Christian learning'. Set off against the Stoic deprecation of
emotion is 'our ethical teaching', which does 'not so much ask
whether the mind of a pious man is angry, as why he is angry'.[85]
Replacing the supposed mediatorial offices of 'good angels'
is the one mediator between God and man, Jesus Christ,[86]
and replacing the sacrifices offered to demons is the participation of the faithful in the self-oblation of Christ as they offer
themselves one body with him in the eucharistic 'sacrifice which
the Church continually celebrates in the sacrament of the
altar'.[87]

Yet in all of this there has been a change of focus, a shift of
concentration. Augustine has achieved a certain detachment
relative to the empire as such both by virtue of his living within
an imperially sponsored Church and by virtue of his conviction
as to the nature and destiny of empires. The shift is away from
the state as a model Church towards the *culture* which his
learned readers represent. The Church offers an alternative to
that whole mode and style of life championed by the learned,
cultured conservatives for whom he writes. In his detachment
from the state he is less moved to adopt its patterns and structures as offering specifications for the life of the City of God.
The adoption of Christianity as the religion of the empire has
not brought any basic difference relative to the origin and end
of this particular Roman province of the earthly city, has not

sacralized the empire nor made it less subject to the nature of earthly empires. The association of the Roman empire with idolatry has been transmuted in Augustine into an association of empire with the most fundamental of all kinds of idolatry, that of pride and lust for rule.

The relation between the earthly and heavenly cities now in the time of the heavenly city's pilgrimage is a relation of 'commingling', 'entanglement'.[88] The two cities are 'mixed'.[89] Augustine simply extends the line of thought which he had initially drawn in controversy with the Donatists. To view the Church as a 'mixed body' is simply one way of specifying the intermingling of the two cities which will continue in this relation until their separation at the final judgement.[90] Augustine maintains a perfectly genuine eschatological reserve, one might say, in being unwilling to draw a line between the two cities which any human being could see. The present mingling of the two cities means that certain members of Babylon even administer the affairs of Jerusalem, as against the Donatists; but it means also that members of Jerusalem will be found administering the affairs of Babylon.[91] So far is Augustine from his pre-Constantian predecessors.

The peace of the earthly city is a positive good and a proper aim of the inhabitants of Jerusalem, as is the right administration of earthly justice. The wise Christian will without question consent to be a magistrate, though he is well aware of the ambiguities and uncertainties attendant upon his office. He enters upon this duty convinced that it would be wickedness to abandon human society.[92] A Christian emperor uses his power to secure the greatest possible extension of the worship of the true God; he is deaf to human praise and flattery, applying severity in the administration of affairs because such is 'necessary to government and to the defence of the republic'. But no Christian ruler may suppose that, because he is a Christian, his necessary exploits will meet with success or that he will be rewarded with temporal prosperity; he is a citizen of the heavenly city.[93] Jerusalem enjoys and 'makes good use' of the peace of Babylon so far as that peace is attainable, but the people of Jerusalem know that their City is ahead and on high, not here.[94]

An elusiveness might strike a modern reader in the passages in which Augustine speaks directly of the relation between the

two cities and of the goals which they pursue—the peace of
eternal blessedness in contemplation of God on the one hand,
and the peace consisting in 'the well-ordered concord of civic
obedience and rule' on the other.[95] It is a delicate matter to
appeal to him either as an authority for the social action of the
twentieth century or for the Spanish Inquisition. We know
from his correspondence how he would take the initiative in
appealing to the secular power for leniency of verdict even upon
Circumcellions convicted of murder, and we know that he could
defend such intervention on the ground that the proper religious
attitude is that men should be loved because they are men.[96]
We find him as an aged man undertaking a journey to the south
of Numidia for the purpose of persuading a general to stay at his
station and so to protect Christian Africa from the incursions
of barbarian nomads.[97] Augustine as Bishop of Hippo and as
frequent visitor to Carthage is a man of affairs deeply involved
in the issues of the day. Yet in *The City of God* he shows, with no
trace of any special accommodation of his views to the tastes
of philosophical readers, how deeply he longs for the final
peace of the eternal city, how thoroughly he has made his own
the Christian Platonist yearning for uninterrupted contemplation in that city of Sion whose very name means 'contemplation'.
The Heavenly City must make use of the peace of this world,
'though only until this mortal lot which has need of it shall
pass away'. A man undertakes a 'righteous activity in affairs'
only because the 'necessity of love' imposes it upon him, and
the implication is, clearly, that if he can sequester himself without anyone imposing this burden and necessity upon him, he is
lucky, free to rejoice in his leisure and in the contemplation of
truth.[98] The tension between the monastic pursuit of contemplation and the active life of affairs is apparent and real. It is an
aspect of the tension between a society with a heavenly destiny
and a society whose end is nothing but death and destruction.

A further aspect of the mingling of the two cities is the problem of imperial repression of heretics. Augustine's developing
attitudes on this subject have been well canvassed and docu-
mented in recent literature, and here there is no need to do more
than summarize. From an early conviction that force would be
entirely inappropriate and that the Donatists could be effectively
dealt with by calm discussion and rational persuasion, Augustine

moved to a view which saw imperial repression of heresy as well as of paganism as one of the 'consolations' which divine providence has procured for the Church amid her many adversities.[99] As early as 395 he had occasion to ponder the success of the Donatists in suppressing under imperial auspices their own schismatics, the Maximianists, though he then still held that force applied to the Donatists would result only in hypocritical conversions. In 405 an edict ordering the dissolution of Donatist churches was the emperor's response to a visit from a once Donatist and now Catholic bishop who had travelled from Africa to Ravenna to display the scars he had received from Circumcellion activists. Augustine's reaction to the effects of this edict was one of growing appreciation. He came to believe that many Donatists had remained in schism either by the hardened indolence of custom or because they had genuinely feared Donatist reprisals were they to become Catholics. Furthermore, his fears as to feigned conversions had been excessive, and had not reckoned with the hidden power of God to use the state's policy of coercion as the occasion of working an inner change of heart. Capital punishment for heresy he never approved, but a policy of sanctions he came, perhaps too easily, to fit into a general view of providence, a providence which works in part by hard restraints imposed upon the wayward hearts of Adam's fallen race. Augustine did not himself initiate or instigate a policy of repression against Donatists. He found himself able to rationalize such a policy once it was under way, and once he had come to view the Donatists less as contentious brothers who needed a bit of talking to, and more as a solid, structured, encampment of the earthly city; from that camp one had to expect not only the ideological warfare of impostors claiming to be the true City of God, but violence as well. It is beside the point to rage against Augustine from the seclusion of an outlook that is far removed from the Roman empire of the fifth century, and it is worth noting that the massive strength of the Donatists as they faced the Catholics does not form a striking parallel to the position of minority groups within medieval Europe.

An essential aspect of Augustine's apologetic project is to display to his cultured readers that the Church of God possesses venerable age and ancient 'authority', the supposed lack of which had long contributed to pagan polemic against the Christians. In Books xv–xviii of *The City of God* he makes it his task to lay out the parallel histories of the two cities from the earliest moment of their earthly contrast. This moment he finds in the conflict between the sons of Adam, the brothers Cain and Abel. It is simply splendid for Augustine's purposes that in the book of Genesis Cain the slayer of his brother is both the first-born son and the builder of the first city. These details fit nicely, first of all, into the general scheme by which Augustine analogizes the community by reference to the individual, a device that is of course as old as Plato's *Republic*. It is the case with each individual that he is first born 'natural', a member of Adam's vitiated race, and then becomes 'spiritual' by grafting into Christ. 'The same thing is true of the entire human race. For at the very start, when the two cities began their history through birth and death, the first to be born was the citizen of this world, and only after him came the pilgrim in this world who belongs to the City of God'.[100] It is this fundamental analogy which, of course, allows Augustine to speak of the Church itself as 'expatriated', 'on pilgrimage'. But second, the story of Cain and Abel allows him to emphasize the essential point that the primary locus of the city of God is in heaven. Cain is the first to build a city. Abel builds none; he is already a member of another city. Third, the biblical story is then of a piece with the general thesis that the 'cities' of this world are as such units of the one earthly city.

Against the background of this scheme Augustine has to tread warily when treating of that earthly city, ancient Israel. Here is a very special case of the 'commingling' of the two cities. Earthly city Israel was, and as such was subject to the vicissitudes and, in A.D. 70, to the final destiny of every earthly city. Yet to this city were entrusted the oracles of God. In the time of the historical existence of Israel the City of God ran its course and made its progress among this people. The root contrast between the two cities within this kingdom was a contrast between those who yearned for carnal happiness in a carnal kingdom and those who desired the future happiness of the kingdom of heaven, and thus a contrast between those who interpreted the divine oracles in each of these directions respectively. The patriarchs and prophets, and an unknown number of others, are members of the City of God, believing in Christ by hope. Yet there is more. The earthly Jerusalem itself was an image, yet only an image, of the heavenly; the kingdom of David, a shadow of a kingdom yet to come. The exile of the Jews in Babylon was a prefiguration of our present exile, the prophets of the exile foreseeing not simply the restoration of the city of Jerusalem, nor yet only Christ and his Church here, but the future liberation which we now await.[101] The City of God has an earthly history, ancient and venerable; those who would despise it for its obscure origins and progress among a people weak and subject to repeated humiliation, are simply blinded by the same pride and bias towards power that turn the incarnate and crucified Christ into an object of contempt.

The history of the two cities runs by parallel, a parallel of both correspondence and contrast. Augustine employs his ingenuity and knowledge through many digressions and to much rhetorical effect, all by way of following out his method of juxtaposition. Here the method seeks to accomplish more than a simple contrast between elements in the total pictures of the two cities. The underlying thesis is that at every crucial, arresting, moment in the history of the earthly city, through the rise and fall of one empire after another, there is to be discerned a moment of equal interest in the progress of the City of God. The divine providence has so arranged things that the original contrast between light and darkness at the creation, i.e. between good and bad angels, is a contrast projected into the history of the world at its beginning and continuing throughout. God has never left darkness without light, be the light ever so hidden from the generality of men. Thus from the midst of Assyria, the most imposing empire before the Roman, came Abraham on his pilgrimage to Canaan—Abraham the faithful to whom the promises were made, in whose lifetime the progress of the City of God 'begins to be more conspicuous'.[102] Moses brought the people of God out of Egypt at the very time that Cecrops ruled Athens, 'in whose reign that city received its name'.[103] The great writing prophets of Israel burst forth upon the world at the very juncture of Assyria's fall and Rome's rise. The whole series builds to the climactic contrast between Augustus and Christ, the latter born, significantly, *after* the reconstituting of the Roman state by its first emperor.[104]

We have seen in this chapter and the previous one how Augustine in a number of ways specifies that the Church holds to its hope in a mode of existence extended through time. Time brings change, a fact that Augustine was able to face with more equanimity than his pagan readers, among whom it was an axiomatic platitude that the permanent is much superior to the changing. Though it is true that the Church possesses a fundamental permanence in its location above and a venerable age through the biblical history, that very history has been the stage of change upon change. The ancient Church offered animal sacrifices which the Church now does not imitate, gloried in a temple which the Church now does not seek to rebuild.[105] Augustine was able to rationalize such details by using the notions of 'image' and 'foreshadowing' in such a way as to make the history of the City of God always a dynamic thrust forward towards closer approximations of the City above and towards richer and more translucent images of that City. Thus the ancient sacrifices were right and proper in their time but in due course were rightly and appropriately sloughed off, being images of the one sacrifice of the Mediator. The hoary theological problem of the relation between the Church of Jesus Christ and old Israel has become to Augustine occasion for suggesting to his pagan conservatives that the total 'progress' of the Church from its earliest days exemplifies the structure of what we today might call 'historical existence'.

That the pilgrim City of God has this kind of history possesses, therefore, apologetic importance. It possesses also the most direct relevance for Augustine's conceptions as a Church theologian. For time brings moral change, forward and backward, as well. It was one of Augustine's chief services to the Western Church, as we have noted, to develop a doctrine of the Church clearly correlated with the problem of sin in just such a way that it made sense to speak of the Church full of sinners. The eschatological pilgrim City of God, *in the narrow sense*, has no citizens other than sinners. The final and most radical application of this doctrine is in the conception, derived probably from Tyconius the Donatist, that the Church now is the millennium. There will be no further 'time' when Christ will come to reign with his saints for a thousand years before the close of history. The saints are now reigning with Christ in the only sense possible before the peace of the supernal City. No life without sin is possible while the saints yet carry this mortal frame and before they put on the resurrection body. Historical time is coextensive with the contrast between earthly and heavenly cities. The reaping angels will separate wheat from tares at the harvest which is the end of the world, not before. Until the end there will be no coming of Christ apart from that coming 'which occurs in his Church throughout the whole of this time, that is, in his members, piece by piece and little by little, since the whole Church is his body'.[106]

With this emphatic stroke Augustine makes it clear that he does not intend his notion of the pilgrim Church to be a notion of a Church any less eschatological than was the perfectionist sense of the Church as the company of saints, already living in the anticipated kingdom. The pilgrim Church and the eschatological Church are one.

5

LEO AND GREGORY:
THE PAPAL PRINCIPATE AND THE
CHURCH IN AFFLICTION

In this chapter we shall direct a rather narrow beam into the writings of two great popes with the intent to discover how Leo and Gregory contribute to themes discussed up to this point.

Leo is of interest for his way of delineating the relation between Church and Empire, for his way of completing the imperial and legal model of the Church in a thoroughly articulated theory of the papacy and for the difficulty one has in integrating these two aspects of his thought. Interpretation of Leo is a peculiarly delicate matter because of the uncertainty in knowing how seriously to take some of the language in which he formulates issues of considerable importance. He is the pope of the mid-fifth century, holding the papal office at a time of acute doctrinal controversy in the Eastern Church and of increasing disorder and uncertainty in the Western Empire. Leo does not yet live at a time when it will seem natural for the popes to turn at least one eye away from the Byzantine emperor and to seek supportive alliances with the rulers of new kingdoms in the West. By instinct and by necessity he sees himself and his Church within the total context of the Christian and Roman Empire, an empire whose political capital and chief ruler are unfortunately at Constantinople, 'New Rome'. In viewing the relation between Church and Empire Leo is noticeably little touched by Augustine's thought concerning the 'two cities'. He does not come close to expressing the view that the Roman Empire is to be regarded as the greatest and most powerful of many empires, all built upon lust for domination and all destined for destruction. His position is, in the end, an imperial one in the sense that he sees Church and Empire as bound together in a mutually supportive relation, each making an indispensable contribution to the goals and well-being of the other. The question then inevitably arises as to the rigour with which one should understand his high language concerning the role of the emperor relative to the Church, holding in view his imposing theory of the Church's papal government.

The position adopted here is to see Leo employing a tissue of traditional imperial conceptions, not usually with the intent of flattering and manipulating the emperor by devious rhetoric, but rather by way of austerely presenting to him his duties as a Christian prince. The intent of rhetoric in letters to official personages of the ancient world is often difficult to gauge as one moves from one writer to another. In the case of Leo the total impact of the corpus of 173 letters (not to speak of the sermons) is an impact from a man of driving determination, courage, and genuine integrity, not to say humourlessness. Rhetoric is there, and 'diplomacy' is there; Leo knows how and when to make his points, and he knows also how to respond to unwelcome events by adopting new tactics. But in summoning the royal persons to their duty in preserving the Church from error and disunity, Leo is not being cynical. It would be more to the point to suggest that the difficulty lies in the consistency of his thought. The worn tissue of imperial conceptions is too frail to withstand the pressure of a bold and newly fashioned theory of the papacy.

The peace and temporal prosperity of the Empire Leo links directly to the peace and unity of the Church. God himself is 'propitiated' by the Church's unity in confessing one faith. The overthrowing of heretics and victory over barbarian enemies are concomitants of one another.[1] In a letter to Theodosius II Leo and his synod of bishops at Rome record their horror over the events at the Council of Ephesus in 449. The council had initiated a temporary victory for the bishop of Alexandria in promoting the orthodoxy of the monk Eutyches, whom Leo now believes to be in heresy through his refusal to admit that there are 'two natures' in Christ. The letter comes to an emphatic close: 'Defend the ingegrity of the Church unshaken against the heretics, so that your empire, too, may be defended by the right hand of Christ.'[2] Underlying this last point is a way of formulating the relation between Church and Empire such that

they are seen as two 'realms' (*imperia*). For certain purposes
Leo can maximize the theme of *two* realms, as we shall notice
below. Important here is to see that he can associate the two
realms so closely in a community of interest that the machina-
tions of the heretics, relative to the peace of the Empire,
constitute a 'civil and pernicious war'. The emperor is to sup-
press this war, knowing that whatever ministers to 'Catholic
freedom' is of direct advantage to the strength of the Empire
itself.[3] A Catholic Church united in the confession of one faith
in one God is an indispensable ingredient in the preservation of
the integrity and well-being of the temporal realm which it is
the business of the emperor to defend against enemies of every
description.[4]

This community of interest between the two realms possesses
relevance not only for imperial policy regarding the Church.
The Church itself sees its own interest as coincident with that
of the Empire. It is not simply that the hand of Christ will
protect the destiny of an empire sponsoring a united Catholic
Church. Conversely, when the faithful see their emperor acting
decisively on behalf of the Church, it is entirely natural that
their prayers be offered to the end that the Empire be 'everywhere extended with glory'.[5] The prayers of the faithful in this
direction are effectual only to the degree that 'the servants of
the one Lord are in no respect separated from the unity of true
peace'.[6] Church and Empire are therefore partners whose
respective interests are locked together.

To Leo it is clear that the emperor acts rightly in rooting
out and deposing heretics from positions of authority in the
Church. It is true that this pope operates with a *revised* version
of the traditional and pagan view that religion is a matter of
imperial policy and that the emperor legitimately, perforce,
acts 'in sacred matters'. But it is of importance to see clearly
the continuity of Leo's conceptions with that ancient view. He
puts the traditional conception to use in summoning the emperor to use his power on behalf of Catholic unity and truth.
The emperor's deposition of the monophysite patriarch of
Alexandria is occasion of rejoicing.[7] Leo encourages the emperor to act not only in situations where it might be said that
ecclesiastical power is wanting and is in need of the force of
imperial arms. The pope knows that the patriarch of Con-

stantinople could, if he wished, depose clerics of Eutychian
views in the church of that city. But Leo, aware of the patriarch's
own heretical sympathies,[8] urges the emperor to do what he
well suspects the patriarch will not do.[9] Imperial power,
though it can be a threat to the Church, can and must be
harnessed to ensure the victory of Catholic peace.

It is against the background sketched above that we must
understand Leo's more particular language concerning the
person of the emperor. The well-being of the Church is directly
linked to the employment of imperial power. We are therefore
not surprised to find Leo summoning to his purpose language
which has the effect of setting the emperor within a providential
ordering of things as a person divinely commissioned. It would
be platitudinous to observe that God wills the well-being of his
Church. To the securing of this end it is necessary that emperors
be raised up who are gifted at least to the degree of being able
correctly to discern the elements of that Catholic faith which it is
their business to defend. In Leo's language we find Christian
and theological vocabulary blending with and yet modifying
the conceptions by which the Roman emperors since Augustus
had seen their rule divinely sanctioned and their persons
divinized. It is to be noted also that Leo's words in this direction
are exactly suited to a time in which succession to the throne no
longer follows reliably from father to son. The military commander Marcian, now raised to the purple and become husband
to the deceased emperor's sister, has been chosen *by God* to his
high office. It is clear that Leo is not interested in any theory of
the divine choosing of secular rulers in and for itself. He, no
more than Augustine, is concerned with systematic reflection
on political theory and the nature of secular rule as such.
Marcian owes his office to the choice of God, but this choosing
is for the precise purpose of defending the Catholic faith against
her enemies.[10]

The emperor is placed in his high office by the grace of God
to the end that he serves as an instrument for the working of
the divine will. Though the emperor is not divinized, the figure
of the hellenistic king acting in concert with God who is 'ruler
of all' stands in the not too distant background. The emperor
is instructed by the Holy Spirit; he is inspired of God.[11] He
possesses an honorary status among the 'preachers of Christ';

his efforts on behalf of the Church are grounds for speaking of his 'priestly and Apostolic mind'. Leo rejoices that the disposition of Theodosius is 'not only that of a king, but even that of a bishop'.[12] Drawing upon traditional Roman conceptions of the 'virtues' which properly characterize the 'best prince (*optimus princeps*)', the pope speaks not infrequently of the virtues attaching to the august rulers, prominent among which are 'trustworthiness (*fides*)', 'piety (*pietas*)', and 'righteousness (*iustitia*)'.[13]

Leo's seriousness in thus speaking of the emperor may be judged from the fact that such language occurs not only in letters directed to the emperors themselves but in letters to ecclesiastics as well, even to Leo's own legates in Constantinople. This consideration, on the other hand, ought not to blind us to Leo's lack of positive interest in imperial ideology for its own sake. Leo cares above all for the state of the Church, and employs elements of imperial ideology in rejoicing over the emperor's beneficent deeds and in warning him of his duties on behalf of the Church. It is misleading to piece together a static mosaic of Leo's imperial language as constituting a theory of empire which Leo has a distinct interest in elaborating and sponsoring. He works within these conceptions with the instinctual sense that Empire and Church belong together in a relation of mutual support. But he knows that the Church has much to regret in past imperial influence and much to guard against in the immediate future, which is why, for example, he is so at pains to insure that his own ecclesiastical authority will predominate at the Council of Chalcedon, in contrast to Ephesus in 449, where Dioscorus, the imperial favourite, presided over the vindication of Eutyches.[14] The same issue is present in a letter written to the emperor six years after Chalcedon; no new council under imperial auspices is to be summoned to reconsider what has been decisively settled there; the emperor is the guardian of the Church, and must simply defend that which has been 'rightly decreed'.[15] To guard and protect the Church is one thing. To rule it is another.

Leo's unguarded and oft cited words in a letter from the year 458 suggesting that the emperor is not able to go astray in his understanding of the faith, are testimony not to any theory of the ruler's infallibility nor to Leo's descent to flattery, but to the

pope's exasperation over the possibility of a new council to
reopen the christological dispute. The emperor has given his
approval to Chalcedon and in doing so has acted in accord with
the see of Peter. That is the fundamental evidence of the
emperor's soundness in the faith, a soundness which it would
now be unthinkable to repudiate.[16] That Leo could allow
himself to speak in this way, however, is evidence of the high
degree of tension present within his espousal both of an imperial
theology and of his theory of the papacy. When the outlook
for orthodoxy appears uncertain in the extreme, Leo carelessly
pushes the language of his imperial theology a step forward by
way of frantically recalling the emperor to his senses.

The issue at stake which the pope never faces head on is the
right of the emperor to summon councils of bishops, a right
which, since Constantine, had formed one of the deepest
presuppositions underlying the ecclesiastical policies of Christian rulers. The history of Leo's manœuvring in the Christological dispute from the year 448 through the next twelve years
is a history of repeated adjustment and newly devised strategies.
Up to the year 451 these strategies are necessary both because
of the acknowledged right of the emperor to call a council[17]
and because of Leo's conviction that he himself should properly
have the controlling hand at any council, whether by its being
convened in Italy[18] where he may preside in person, or by the
sending of legates who will preside in his stead.[19] His line is to
regard the doctrinal issue as having been settled by his dogmatic letter to Flavian,[20] the famous tome, and to look upon
the coming council as essentially an occasion not of open debate
about matters of the faith, but of judgement upon Eutyches and
his supporters.[21] Once the Council of Chalcedon has met in
451 and has given its endorsement to his tome, no further
opening of the dogmatic issue is conceivable. Besides, Leo
knows that his legates had not in fact presided at Chalcedon[22]
and would probably not do so at any further council held in
the East. He had none the less achieved an important victory
in the Council's acceptance of the tome, a victory which he had
no desire to see placed in danger. These are the dynamics of
the situation prompting the pope to write to the emperor in
458 that no error can possibly delude his faith. The tension
between the Church whose protector is the emperor and the

Church whose ruler is the pope has tightened almost to the point of shattering.

Leo's doctrine of the papacy is to be seen not simply as a doctrine about the relation of the pope to the churches of Christendom but also as a doctrine about the relation between Church and Empire. Leo brings to a culminating point a history of tactical manœuvre and fragmentary theorizing that had marked the bishopric of Rome from the second century onward and which had gathered momentum in the fourth century. The recognition of Christianity under Constantine and its subsequent elevation to the status of religion of the Empire had raised acutely the problem of the autonomy of the Church. The papacy emerges as a Western answer to this problem. In the East the autonomy of the Church was not seen as a problem requiring either theoretical or institutional solution. The assumption there was that the Church's relation to the State was a relation of the same type as had normally characterized the peoples of antiquity and their ethnic religions. The Church was absorbed into the State, both together forming one organically united people of God. This does not mean that we are to apply uncritically the label 'Caesaropapism'. The history of the Church in the Byzantine Empire is generously supplied with events, individuals and groups, all bearing testimony to a recurring willingness on the part of Eastern Christians to influence or to oppose the emperor on religious and theological grounds. In the East religious opposition to the emperor tends to take the shape of a very traditional political factionalism within a total society understood to be Christian.

The papal theory which we see reaching a marked degree of crystallization in Leo, on the other hand, has deep roots in a Western concept which sees the Church as a society offering both a contrast and a parallel to the structures of civil society. We have seen differing ways in which this concept comes to expression in Tertullian, Cyprian, and Augustine. In Cyprian in particular we observed how a theological mind deeply informed by principles of Roman law viewed the Church as a society whose unity, peace, and concord it is the function of bishops to guarantee and preserve. There are now two obvious and crucial differences between Cyprian and Leo. Cyprian wrote in conditions of the Church's mortal combat with a

K

persecuting empire, and Cyprian's theory of the government of the Church is an entirely collegial one, no bishop being placed in analogy to the emperor. The first of these differences turns out as of less importance than might have been imagined. Leo is in a different kind of competition with the emperor. He has to preserve the Church not from disintegration and disunity at the hands of an anti-Christian emperor, but from the violation of its divinely given constitution at the hands of a Christian emperor having no authority to 'rule' the Church. Complementary to this problem is Leo's awareness of a responsibility to oversee the Church of the West within a political context in which imperial administration is growing weaker and the bishop is emerging with many attributes of a local ruler. We have seen that Leo thinks within the framework of an imperial theology in which the emperor occupies a place of central importance. It now becomes of crucial urgency to him to lay bare the divinely given constitution of the spiritual *imperium* which is the Church,[23] and in particular to make clear the nature and warrants of the authority which in the Church stands parallel to the emperor in the temporal *imperium*. He does this by drawing heavily upon the language and conceptions of Roman imperial law, restating and systematizing a conception of the papal office that had made giant strides forward in the writings and utterances of popes over a period of some sixty years before Leo took office in 440. We shall here offer the barest outline of Leo's papal theory.

The plenary powers of the pope rest upon plenary powers given in the first instance to the Apostle Peter, who received such powers for his merit in having been the first of the Apostles to confess Jesus as the Christ, in the famous incident at Caesarea Philippi.[24] To Peter is entrusted the government of the Church.[25] This government includes both jurisdictional and doctrinal elements. Jurisdictionally it means that Peter receives the 'power of binding and loosing', complete authority over all disciplinary matters regulating the holding of Church offices and the conditions upon which men either are or are not in communion with the Church.[26] Doctrinally Peter founded the teaching of the Christian Church 'by his uniform preaching throughout the world'.[27] The unique role of Peter is further defined in his relation both to Christ and to the other Apostles.

In bestowing upon Peter his commission, Christ takes Peter up into an 'undivided union' with himself;[28] Christ the Rock ordains that Peter also be Rock made solid by Christ's own strength, 'so that those things which are proper to my own power might be common to you by participation with me'.[29] Relative to the other Apostles Peter possesses the 'principate'.[30] Leo makes the crucial distinction, quite alien to Cyprian's equally juristic view of the matter: the Apostles possess a common *honor* (that of the episcopal order) but not an identical *potestas* (jurisdictional power).[31] A scheme of derivative government is outlined whereby the authority given by Christ to Peter is in turn bestowed by Peter upon the Apostles, but bestowed in such a way that the authority of Peter is not temporary but permanent. 'The privilege of Peter remains.' Peter in an immediate sense rules all of the Church's pastors, whom Christ rules in a more ultimate and prior sense.[32]

To have said so much is to have passed imperceptibly into Leo's language about the papacy itself, for Peter lives and governs in each succeeding occupant of the papal chair. 'Peter has not abandoned the government of the Church which he undertook.'[33] The notion of the transferral of Peter's plenary powers to succeeding popes Leo fixes by the heavily legal conception of inheritance. The pope is the heir (*haeres*) of Peter. From a legal point of view the difference between the heir and the deceased is nil, the one succeeding to the total rights possessed by the other. The pope is moreover an 'unworthy heir', a formula which allows Leo to distinguish between the person and the office which he holds. In the case of Peter's successors they inherit the office of the prince of the Apostles while not possessing that particular merit which had been the ground of his receiving it in the first place. Thus does the pope function 'in the place' of Peter.[34] The Roman Church possesses the 'principate over all the churches of the whole world'.[35] Because of the peculiar relation of Peter to Christ, Leo can consistently say that whatever he as pope rightly does is done by Christ himself.[36]

This monarchical and legal theory of papal authority has the effect of rendering *partially* obsolete a number of older arguments upon which the authority of the bishop of Rome had been thought to rest. Once a theory has been adopted which concen-

trates upon a legal jurisdiction conferred by the inheritance of
a principate, it is no longer quite so relevant to appeal to such
historical details as the death of Peter in Rome, the presence
of Peter's tomb in Rome, the founding of the Roman Church
by Peter, or even the succession of the pope to Peter's *episcopal*
office in Rome. The bishop of Antioch, it might be argued,
succeeded to a Petrine episcopal office in that city. The important fact for Leo is not that he stands in succession of office to
Peter as a bishop; the other Apostles were also bishops. Of
crucial significance is the succession to Peter's office as 'prince'
of the Apostles and as primate of the universal Church. Though
this much is true, the question might still be asked, How does
one know that it is the occupant of the see of Rome who suc-
ceeds to this office? The force of this question is simply to suggest
that Leo's theory is not so abstracted from historical arguments
concerning the relation of Peter to the church at Rome as has
been sometimes thought in recent scholarship. Leo's theory is
formulated against the background of these older arguments
and continues to derive some measure of its force from them.
He does not himself give us a clear answer to the question just
posed, unless it be assumed that the successor to Peter's episcopal office in Rome is *ipso facto* the successor to Peter's primatial
office.

Leo appears clearly to make this assumption, and in fact the
distinction between a Petrine episcopal office and a Petrine
primatial office is much more a creation of subsequent theorizing than it is present in the writings of Leo. The progression
of thought in his mind may be formulated as follows: Peter,
having founded the Church of Antioch, went to Rome because
of the inherent appropriateness of his being at the seat of
Empire as prince of the Apostles; from that point he could more
effectively spread the light of his teachings 'throughout the
body of the world'; thus located at the city which was already
'head' of the world in a secular sense, he established there his
own proper (primatial) see which in spiritual terms is also to
be described as 'head of the world'; thenceforth Peter is in
Peter's see in the persons of successive popes.[37]

It will have been observed that Leo's argument is not at all
divorced from the theme of the secular eminence of the city
of Rome at the time of Peter's residence there. The tension

between New Rome and Old Rome in Leo is one in which 'non-theological factors' are far from absent.

We are now in a better position to understand why Leo is so nervous about councils called to meet in the East under immediate imperial influence, and why he is so concerned to limit and direct the agenda of such councils. 'Things secular stand on a different basis from things divine.'[38] For precisely this reason the notorious twenty-eighth canon of the Council of Chalcedon is unacceptable; it suggests that the reason for Rome's eminence in the Church is simply that it was the imperial city and assigns to Constantinople, New Rome, 'equal rank in matters ecclesiastical', holding second place only to old Rome. Let the new royal city be ever so glorious, imperial glory cannot make it an apostolic see.[39] The theme of papal rule as not dependent upon secular rulers makes its appearance in another interesting context, the famous rescript issued in the names of those secular rulers Theodosius II and Valentinian III in regard to Leo's drastic measures in regulating the stormy affairs of the church of southern Gaul. The wording of the rescript is quite possibly due to the influence of Leo himself. It states exactly what he believed: the judgement of the Roman see would have been valid throughout Gaul 'even without imperial sanction, for what limit can there be to the authority of so great a bishop in the churches'.[40]

While Leo sees Church and Empire contributing reciprocally to their mutual well being, their relations are in fact the relations of two *imperia*, the one a 'spiritual', the other a secular. The spiritual has its centre at old Rome; the Apostle Peter, having gone to that city precisely because it was the imperial city, made it to be the 'head of the whole world' by founding there his apostolic see.[41] Constantinople by Leo's standards can in comparison make no more claim to eminence than could old Rome before it had been dignified by the presence of the apostolic see. The two *imperia* are thus distinguished by two capitals in continual tension. That, we may say, is Leo's doctrine of the two cities.

In the writings of Gregory the Great at the end of the sixth century we discover a complex amalgam of conceptions from at least three sources: the thought of Augustine, monastic spirituality, and the papal tradition coming from Leo and modified to a degree by the exigencies of events in the sixth century. Gregory's thought occurs within a context of severe dislocation and uncertainty, both political and ecclesiastical. The Italian peninsula in mid-sixth century had known the devastation of the emperor Justinian's military campaign to regain Italy for the empire from the hands of the Ostrogoths. Thereafter Byzantine Italy was governed by an imperial functionary, the Exarch, from his residence in Ravenna. But scarcely a decade and a half after the last victory over the Ostrogoths in 554, the Lombards were making their presence felt in northern Italy and were beginning to conquer, city by city, the northern part of the peninsula. By 593, the third year of Gregory's pontificate, the Lombard king Agilulf was besieging Rome, a trial prodigal of misery graphically portrayed in the pope's homilies on the prophet Ezekiel. Though, after some weeks of siege, the Lombards retreated northwards, the ordeal served for Gregory as the crowning evidence of imperial weakness and inconstancy in Italy. The early 590s saw drought, famine, and plague on a gigantic scale.

The ecclesiastical situation in the West was complicated not only by the traditional Arianism of the Gothic tribes, but also by schism in Gaul and northern Italy in reaction from the Council of Constantinople's condemnation in 553 of the 'Three Chapters', i.e. writings of Theodore of Mopsuestia, Theodoret, and Ibas; the Western schismatics were convinced that in approving this action the papacy had been party to a renunciation of the Christology of Chalcedon and had in fact if not in words accommodated itself to Monophysitism. Theodelinda, Catholic queen of the Lombards, though a powerful ally in Gregory's efforts towards a truce between Lombards and empire, caused him deep pain in going over to the cause of the schismatics and thus giving renewed impetus to their cause. And there was the continuing irksome claim of the patriarch of Constantinople that he should be called 'universal bishop', a claim which in Gregory's time was not new but which he resisted with great animus.

These facts will serve to suggest that Gregory's pontificate was a time of severe stress on more than one front. The multiple strains which he sensed are to be directly related to the high pitch of eschatological expectancy which are everywhere apparent in his writings; he is convinced that the end of all things is at hand.

Gregory assumes and in part repeats the general doctrine of papal authority that had been formulated by Leo, though without the precision of Leo's legal vocabulary.[42] Two modifications are present, however, which are not without importance.

The Western schismatics hold the papacy highly suspect over the issue of the Three Chapters, both because of present papal policy in upholding the condemnation and because of the unedifying vacillations of the weak pope Vigilius on the subject in the years 543–53, not to speak of the like vacillation of Vigilius' one-time deacon and successor in the papal office, Pelagius i. How could one any longer take seriously the assertion of Pope Hormisdas (514–23) that the Christian religion had always remained pure in the Roman Church? The sixth-century papacy, partly out of embarrassment over its changing policies, developed a defence of its final position not in appeal so much to the authority of the pope as definer of doctrine, but in appeal to the consensus of the several apostolic sees, all of which were united in accepting the decisions of the Council of Constantinople as well as those of the previous four ecumenical councils. Gregory continues this line of defence, changing it slightly. Rome adheres to the first four ecumenical councils as well as to the condemnation of the Three Chapters at Constantinople, Rome does this in concert with the patriarchs of the East, and the combined weight of the Roman see of Peter with the councils and the other patriarchs is evidence that Rome represents the faith of the 'universal Church'.[43] Gregory rests his case with the appeal to a universality which is perceivable in the concerted testimony of these witnesses.

Second, in his efforts to win support in the East for his opposition to the title 'universal bishop' as applying to the patriarch of Constantinople or to any other bishop, Gregory expands the conception, 'see of Peter': Peter was responsible for the founding of the sees of both Antioch and Alexandria, the former by founding it himself and labouring there for seven years, the latter through sending his own disciple, Mark the evangelist; though the Apostle 'raised on high' the Roman see by his martyrdom there, the three sees constitute one Petrine see over which the bishops of the three cities preside.[44]

Gregory sees it as his business to intervene directly in the affairs of churches outside his own metropolitan jurisdiction only for purposes of upholding canonical procedures, settling disputes, and correcting abuses.[45] While it is impossible to include all of Gregory's actions in a precise theory of the modes of papal jurisdiction, generally it is the case that in his intervention in affairs of the Western churches he was free in taking or in urging precise disciplinary and jurisdictional action, while to the churches of the East he made his will known through admonitory and more general letters to the patriarchs. It is clear to Gregory that to him has been entrusted 'the care of the whole Church'.[46] The exercise of this care he undertakes as the circumstances of the situation will allow, making clear that he does not wish to usurp either the proper functions of local bishops or the traditional privileges of the more principal sees, and combining a passionate desire for the right government of the Church with a most winning humility—he is the 'servant of the servants of God'.[47]

That Gregory conceives the Church on the model of a unified *imperium* is evident in many ways, not the least of which is of course the notion of the principate attaching to the see of Peter. Corresponding to the three traditional 'orders' of society in the Empire—senators, equestrians, and plebs—are three 'orders' in the Church: the rulers (i.e. bishops), the continent, and the married.[48] Gregory wants to draw a close analogy between secular rulers and bishops, as the title of his celebrated work on the duties of the episcopate might suggest: *Liber Regulae Pastoralis*. A bishop is the 'Lord's Anointed'; he is a 'throne of God'; as Saul was to ancient Israel, so is a bishop to his church. The 'subjects' of ecclesiastical rulers owe to them the same awesome respect paid to secular rulers.[49] Language such as this takes on heightened significance when it is placed in its historical context and is seen as applying to bishops who did in fact play roles of actual secular rule, in acting as local magistrates, in the oversight of the distribution of food, and in the defence of cities against invaders. Gregory the Roman patriot takes the lead in this regard; he plays a key role in the defence of the city of Rome and makes up for the weakness and lassitude of the

Exarch by himself appointing military governors to other cities in Italy. He on the one hand encourages bishops to undertake civil responsibilities out of necessity but on the other hand laments two dire effects of this necessity: bishops too easily assume airs of inflated authority inappropriate to their spiritual office, and they do not devote themselves to their proper office of preaching. The repeated theme in Gregory's writings of the urgent duty of bishops to preach the gospel is a continual reminder not only of one of Gregory's chief interests but of a crucial problem of the Western episcopate in his day.[50]

An essential part of the picture is the papal patrimony. Here is not the place to recount the details of Gregory's administrative zeal in the management of these vast and scattered estates for the employment of the poor, relief of the hungry, and protection of the oppressed. We must be content to call attention to the fact that the patrimony both contributed to the model of the Church as *imperium* and at the same time contributed to the blurring of the distinction between a 'spiritual' and a 'secular' *imperium*. The patrimony of Peter is a clear and quite 'secular' parallel to the estates which constituted the patrimony of the emperor and whose proceeds went directly to the imperial treasury. In the administration of the patrimony Gregory employs clerics whose titles are all drawn from the vocabulary of imperial administration—*rector, defensor, chartularius, notarius*.[51] These officials are directly appointed by the pope, invested solemnly with their office in Rome, and serve extracurricular duties as papal informants on local bishops.[52] As agents stationed permanently in the various localities where lands of the patrimony are to be found, they make an important contribution to the pope's knowledge and oversight of the Church at large. So long as we are drawing parallels, we might note also that Gregory finds it repeatedly necessary to correct among his agents just the sort of administrative abuse—fraud, violence, unjust seizure of property and persons—that had long brought odium upon the imperial administration.

Gregory's relation to the Byzantine emperor is one of repeated tension and frustration. Coming from a senatorial family and presiding over a city which still owes allegiance to the 'Roman' emperor, Gregory knows himself to be a subject of that ruler. There are clear marks of his thinking within the

context of the kind of imperial theology characteristic of Leo.
The Empire is the 'holy republic'.[53] The peace and integrity
of the republic depend upon the peace and integrity of the
Church.[54] Sovereignty is bestowed upon the emperor by God
'in order that the temporal kingdom may serve the heavenly
kingdom'.[55] By the enacting of laws for the well-being of the
Church the ruler engages in his own mode of 'preaching the
faith'.[56] The notion of the respect due to a bishop as the Lord's
anointed is based, as we saw above, upon a prior notion of the
respect due to the secular ruler.

If the emperor undertakes actions relative to the Church of
which the pope disapproves, Gregory's tactic is to reprove the
ruler but to obey so far as his conscience will allow him to
believe that he may do so 'without sin'.[57] But when he may
not comply without sin in the case of the emperor's wishing to
depose uncanonically a bishop in the imperial diocese of
Illyricum, an area of recurring tension in relations between
popes and emperors, Gregory makes clear his unwillingness to
take the final step of open breach with the emperor; he says
only that he will not be implicated in such a proceeding.[58] The
edict from the emperor Maurice ordering that no one engaged in
duties either of public administration or of military service
may retire into a monastery, prompted a letter from pope to
ruler highly characteristic of Gregory's stance: the edict, in
forbidding earthly soldiers to become soldiers of Christ, is in
direct contravention of the divinely ordained relation of
Empire to Church; the earthly kingdom properly serves the
heavenly kingdom; Gregory none the less, out of obedience to
the emperor, has caused the hateful law to be transmitted to
'various parts of the world'; and in protesting to his emperor
Gregory has discharged his obligation to God.[59] This pope
does not push his papal theory to the point of open declaration
of war in defending his divinely given right over the spiritual
imperium.

It is clear in fact that Gregory's deference to secular rulers
is not simply a function of his position relative to the *Byzantine*
emperor. One of the notable aspects of his life and thought is
his clear-headed perception that the new barbarian kingdoms
of the West are not a mere, ephemeral nightmare in the career
of the Empire but a permanent political fact requiring serious

reckoning. When the pope turns his attention to the regulation of ecclesiastical matters in the Frankish kingdoms, he simply applies to the rulers of those kingdoms fundamental assumptions underlying the relation between the Church and the Roman emperors. It is the secular rulers who are to assemble synods for the suppression of simony and who are otherwise to see to the proper ordering of Church affairs; it is Catholic kings who 'labour in the gathering of souls for the profit of the heavenly kingdom'.[60]

We gain a different perspective upon Gregory's thought on the Church when we turn to the immense commentary, running to thirty-five books, which he wrote on the book of Job: the famous *Moralia*. The work is commonly cited as exemplifying Gregory's penchant for allegorical exegesis of Scripture, which indeed it does, at tiresome length. Or it is said to express a spiritual and ascetic theology having its roots in Eastern monastic spirituality mediated to Gregory by such a figure as John Cassian, a judgement which is entirely reasonable so far as it goes. But one does not gain access to the heart of this work until one has taken Gregory seriously at his word that the figure of Job represents the Church. In the pedantic jargon of our day we might say that the *Moralia* offers the great pope's phenomenological account of existence in the Church. The Church is displayed as the suffering Church. It is difficult to think of a scriptural narrative more appropriate to Gregory's sense of the Church's crisis and trial at the close of the sixth century than that of Job. Job is a type both of Christ and of the Church and in this dual role signifies the suffering of Christ, the suffering of the Church, and the union of the two in their suffering.[61] The problem of Job's being or not being a sinner, moreover, offers Gregory opportunity to explore anew the old question of the relation between sin and the Church as eschatological community. The designation of Job's friends as heretics[62] is a sign of Gregory's continuing worries over Arians, neo-Nestorians, Monophysites, and Donatists. The *dramatis personae* are completed in Job's wife, who represents the carnally minded within the Church,[63] and in Elihu, who personifies the 'proud' in the Church'.[64] Within this group of relationships is set the problem of the elect over against the reprobate within the Church. It is manifest throughout that Gregory's mind has been deeply informed by the problems and thought of Augustine,[65] and that he has not embraced the full Augustinian doctrine of predestination. He modifies Augustine's teaching, chiefly under the influence of monastic spirituality. Once the reader has perceived something of the structure of issues determining the thought of the *Moralia*, it becomes an engaging opus, most revealing of the pressures at work in the mind and heart of its distinguished author.

Here we shall be content to call attention to three issues of central importance in Gregory's reflections on the suffering Church: the problem of power and pride, the theme of contemplation, and the question of the elect.

In both his letters and in the *Moralia*, Gregory shows himself constantly preoccupied with the problem of 'power' in relation to the Church. Gregory the first monk to become pope is captured by Benedictine humility. He is both the first biographer of Benedict and an avid reader of Augustine; in his thought flow together from these two sources the themes of detachment from the things of this world and of the antithesis between love of God and love of power over men. The lifting up of self over others is one of the chief signs of the working of Satan in the world and in the Church. The massive intrusion into the Church of the lust for power is itself a sign of the imminent coming of the man who is Antichrist for the final struggle between light and darkness before the end of all things. The antithesis between Christ and Satan Gregory repeatedly draws as an antithesis between Christ with his body the Elect Church and Satan with his 'body'. A central aspect of the suffering of the Church is trial at the hands of those who care chiefly for worldly glory and who manipulate the body of Christ to serve their satanic desires. The tension between Christ and Antichrist is heightened by the fact that Antichrist, when he comes, unites in himself both the power of this world and 'apparent holiness'. Gregory sees himself living at a time when smoke comes from the nostrils of Antichrist before he appears openly.[66]

In the *Moralia* these teachings are cast for the most part in general terms. It is not difficult, however, to correlate such themes there with concrete events and issues appearing in the pope's letters. It is clear that Gregory has in mind both the relation between the Church and temporal rulers and also those who hold powerful positions within the Church. A highly visible case is of course the patriarch of Constantinople's claim to the title 'universal bishop'. When writing to the patriarch, Gregory alludes to the connivance of the court, laying a large part of the blame upon 'secular persons' who have prompted the bishop to his satanic effrontery; when writing to the court, he denounces the pride of his brother bishop as a sign that the times of Antichrist are near.[67] The identical issue is present in numerous other letters in which Gregory will warn an ecclesiastic to do his duty in care of the poor even against the will of local rulers,[68] will rebuke a powerful agent of the papal patrimony for being party to the rebellion of local clergy against their bishop,[69] and will reprimand a bishop of Ravenna for lusting after secular dignity by wearing the pallium in street processions.[70] Gregory has deeply absorbed the Augustinian doctrine of the interpenetration of the earthly and heavenly cities. This interpenetration has become for him more acutely agonizing than it had been for Augustine, for at least three reasons: he is a monk become pope who, on one side of his mind, thinks within the framework of an imperial theology foreign to Augustine; he lives amidst political disorder and social misery requiring ecclesiastics to assume heavy duties of secular administration; and he presides over a patrimony generating just the kind of problems relative to the power of this world which he sees as constituting a serious threat to the life of the spirit.

A second and closely related aspect of the trial of the Church in Gregory's mind has to do with the distraction between the contemplative life and the active. Gregory adopts the thesis, characteristic of Eastern ascetic theology, that man was originally created for a life in contemplation of God and that his banishment from paradise involved him in the loss of the power of contemplation. The Incarnation restores to man this lost power, and it is in the monastic life that contemplation leading to the vision of God is chiefly nurtured. The future life in the heavenly kingdom will be one in which the saints will enjoy an uninterrupted vision of God. Thus monasticism has a clearly eschatological significance as the context within which the life of the future is anticipated, though the vision of God here is always a partial and passing one. The life of contemplation is

not only an eschatological good in itself. It is also a means for
the conquering of 'fleshly' life; some men in fact are unable to
detach themselves from the damning lust for the things of this
world unless they 'give up all things' and enter the monastery.
The life of monastic detachment and contemplation, therefore,
has a twofold importance: it is the context where future blessedness is in a way brought into the present, and for some it is an
indispensable means of final salvation. A flourishing monasticism is therefore essential for the Church, and it is no wonder
that Gregory took such pains for the endowment and protection
of monasteries.[71]

'Quiet' is essential to the life of monks, so essential, for
example, that Gregory will not allow a baptistry to be built in
a monastery;[72] disturbances from the outside world, even in the
form of public occasions of worship, are disallowed. But Gregory
on the other hand is prodigal in his employment of monks for
service in the Church at large—as local pastors, missionaries,
administrators of the patrimony, and papal legates. He chooses
such men for these tasks because the necessity of times and
places demands their services.[73] They are men who have
achieved an inner tranquillity such that they can keep their
mind on their essential business and not be distracted by the
temptations and blandishments of the world.[74] Responding to
the demands of charity on behalf of the body of Christ, they
came forth from their lives of contemplation, taking as their
model Christ himself who made himself 'lower than the angels'
and assumed the form of man.[75]

That all seems straightforward enough, but it is not the end
of the matter. A continuing uneasiness disturbs Gregory on this
subject. The association in his mind of monastic contemplation
with the eschatological goal of the Church can lead him even
to speak as if those given to the monastic life are themselves the
elect.[76] Gregory does not in the end really mean this, as a
number of passages make clear,[77] but the fact that he can even
suggest it reveals how centrally important the monastic life is
to his conception of the Church; to live in monastic contemplation is right now to live the life which will very soon be the
privilege of all the elect. This is Gregory's solution to the problem of the eschatological perfection of the Church. It is contemplative monks who are 'holy men'. In order that the Church

be the Church, it is necessary that some be leading this life
now. As has frequently been noticed, Gregory severely modifies
the Augustinian doctrine of election so as to teach that even the
elect can sink into perdition permanently by a failure of will.
When we now recall that some men require the life of contemplation in order to be saved at all, we can understand why the
necessity that some monastics leave the contemplative life for
active service in the Church should be so productive of anxiety
in Gregory's mind. The pressures attendant upon the life of
active service sometimes succeed in utterly distracting a
mind that could maintain its serenity if it stayed within the
cloister.[78]

We are able to observe Gregory himself as 'exhibit A' of this
anxiety. He tells us that in leaving the monastery and assuming
the papal office he has been banished from the face of his
Maker; the ascent to the topmost summit of rule in the Church
has been a fall from the lofty height of contemplative tranquillity, a fall which has brought upon him deep groanings of
spirit and dark shadows of grief.[79] The occupant of the papal
throne has suffered shipwreck in his loss of quietude; after nine
years of labour in that office he fears lest he may not after all
reach his heavenly port.[80] Yet he is certain that the risk is worth
it. The ground of this certitude is an eschatological one. He lives
at the end of the age; 'through many tribulations we must
enter into the Kingdom of God'.[81] Whereas for Augustine the
hidden counsels of God were of importance in pondering the
mystery of election and the fall of men once faithful who are
yet reprobate, in Gregory those counsels are much more important in pondering the mystery of the calling of monastics
from contemplation into active service as the end of time
approaches.[82]

Scholars have long called attention to the fact that though
Gregory uses a large part of the Augustinian vocabulary
concerning the predestination of the elect, his doctrine of
election is not that of Augustine, nor is it easy to draw together
any coherent doctrine of predestinating election from his
writings. Though he does not explicitly take issue with Augustine,
his implicit question to the great doctor is essentially that of the
monastics with whom Augustine had to deal in his own lifetime. It is the question of the reality of moral struggle relative

to freedom of will. His own answer is that grace, though it anticipates every human movement towards God and is bestowed without regard to prior merits, none the less requires the genuinely free co-operation of the human will in order that its work may be accomplished. Men may or may not 'follow' grace; the good works of the faithful are both God's and their own. Gregory teaches a genuinely synergistic doctrine.[83] Though severe difficulties remain in respect of the coherence of Gregory's thought, it is clear that he both wished to retain the category, 'elect', and introduced a serious modification into the Augustinian scheme. The elect are those whom God will finally save, and their number is fixed.[84]

We have seen that Augustine had to labour against much opposition in establishing his thesis that saints are in this life sinners and also that this very thesis, serious as it was both for him and his opponents, could serve as one of his arguments for defending the righteousness of God in condemning some of the faithful to reprobation. In Gregory the theme of the elect as sinners is on its way to being a platitude, but only on its way. He repeats it many times,[85] sometimes adding the essentially monastic and ascetic point that the sins of the elect are internal sins of thought.[86] But of whatever sort they are, the sins of the elect are hateful to God. An essential difference in emphasis between Augustine and Gregory, of importance equal to that concerning the meaning of 'election', is that Gregory sees himself and the Church over which he presides as living at the very edge of that end time which Augustine in the closing books of *The City of God* had seen as still lying somewhere indefinitely ahead. The suffering of Job is the eschatological suffering of the elect;[87] the suffering of the elect is the execution of judgement upon their remaining sins;[88] the present season of the Church's grief is immediately preparatory to the joy which shall follow hereafter.[89]

The sufferings of which Gregory speaks are of a manifold sort. They include the intrusion and the temptations of worldly power, and the anxiety over the contemplative life, to which we have called attention. They include, obviously, the barbarian devastations,[90] and the plague and famine. The political and military power of heretical, i.e. Arian and neo-Nestorian, Christians in the West was particularly galling to Gregory.[91]

But one of the chief forms of 'persecution' to which the elect are subject is the presence within 'holy Church' of the reprobate, who receive the Church's sacraments but are in fact hypocrites, and who cannot withstand the pressures of the present times.[92] Gregory believes the reprobate to be a majority within the Church.[93] The providential function of the reprobate within the Church is to act as a source of temptation; they provide occasions by which the faith and steadfastness of the elect are tried and purified.[94] The theme of corrective, educational, punishment is thus clearly present in Gregory's reflection upon the suffering of the elect.[95] But of such punishment Gregory is quite genuinely fearful. It can 'scarcely now be borne', the ferocity of it today suggesting how terrible will be the punishing wrath of God at the last day tomorrow.[96]

The loosening of Augustine's doctrine of election simply contributes to the white-hot pitch of eschatological expectancy. Gregory sees the company of the elect as already entering upon a final contest with satanic power whose final outcome, as it affects any single person, is known but not ordained by God. The antithesis of elect and reprobate within the Church, conditioned as it is by ascetic and perfectionist spirituality, is not unlike the antithesis of Church and world in Tertullian and Cyprian, who also looked for a speedy end of all things. The Judgement which has already begun requires the vigorous exercise of a moral freedom guaranteed by God the judge. Perfectionism, freedom, and the imminent end are again found united, though united within the scenario, let us say, of Augustine's pilgrim Church travelling to its heavenly home.[97]

Gregory's writings can be seen as offering interesting confirmation of a thesis emphasized but not originated by recent sociologists of religion, viz., that intense expectation of an imminent and cataclysmic end of all things at the hands of an avenging deity is a recurring characteristic of religious folk who find themselves oppressed by hostile power. The point has of course obvious application to Tertullian and Cyprian, writing under the threat of pre-Constantinian persecution. It is perhaps unusual to view the 'great' pope Gregory in this light as well, but surely it is right to do so. Centuries of the triumphalist spirit should not be allowed to obscure from us the actual

L

position of Gregory at the turn of the seventh century. The fact that in Gregory's case the specific agents exercising hostile power appear to be various does not really detract from this thesis. Gregory, seeing himself as peculiarly responsible for the well being of the whole Church, senses a threat to the Church of any kind and in any quarter as a threat of a kind to himself. The particular embodiments of hostile power, moreover, with which he is preoccupied share the characteristic, of supreme and vexing importance to him, that they are outward professors of Christian faith: Christian emperors at Constantinople, who variously turn their backs upon the defence of Catholic Italy, prevent imperial servants from becoming monks, unlawfully depose a bishop, and support the pretensions of the bishop in their capital; that bishop himself, claiming a universal episcopate over the Church; the Arian invaders of Italy; the neo-Nestorian schismatics, latterly rejuvenated by the adherence of the Lombard queen; bishops and even papal agents who cannot resist the temptation to exploit the powerless and to affect the posture and manners of power. The mythic figure of the Antichrist, assuming both the oppressive power of this world and the aura of holiness, binds all of these into a unity. The presence of the 'world' as reprobate within the Church, the commingling of the two cities with their two loves, has now, for Gregory the pope within a nominally Christian 'holy republic', brought upon the Church the suffering of the final eschatological woes and has brought the city of man to the edge of the last abyss.

Gregory's heart was in the monastery, in pursuit of the perfection of contemplation. His destiny was to sit at the pinnacle of ecclesiastical responsibility in the Western Church under conditions of severe trial. The contrast between the ideal of perfection and the condition of the Church with its attendant challenges was productive of the tensions, anxieties, and cataclysmic expectations manifest in Gregory's writings. But the same conflict was productive also of the novel and creative policy which Gregory undertook in his deployment of trusted monks on missions of high moment, supremely exemplified in his dispatch of a group of monks under the leadership of one Augustine for the purpose of converting the heathen English. In making this move, so full of consequence for the history of medieval Europe, Gregory displayed, among other things, a recurring trait of those who have entertained vivid (eschatological expectations: though the end of the world is near, the future of the Church in the world must none the less be planned for.)

CONCLUSION

Here I wish briefly to set out some summary reflections which are intended in part to draw together materials studied in the foregoing chapters and in part to suggest a few points of relevance which these materials might possess for the Church today. I should have felt deeply remiss if I had left the latter topic out of view entirely, though what will be offered here does not begin to be exhaustive.

The authors whom we have studied in this book represent what might be called the great tradition in Western patristic theology. [The Church as an object of reflection is central to their attention.] This centrality is a function of two recurring themes: the Church as eschatological community; and the Church as one, 'spiritual', society standing as both a parallel and a contrast to the temporal society of the Roman Empire. In brief, the Church is holy and one; and its unity and holiness affect and condition one another. The recurring prominence of the problem of the unity of the Church in Western thought reflects a continuing search to discover an empirical identity that is by hypothesis not given by the institutions of the secular state, though the language and conceptions for expressing this identity are in large part given by the forms, political and otherwise, of secular society.

In Tertullian the unity of the Church is first chiefly defined, against the Gnostic threat, as a unity of faith whose apostolicity is guaranteed by the succession of bishops. The eschatological holiness of the Church is a problem so intense as to lead Tertullian into Montanist perfectionism. It is this holiness which prompts the spirit of Christian separatism, expressing itself in the life and structures of a society which stand over against the life and structures of pagan society. The unity of the Church is therefore a unity of faith plus a unity of the Spirit who seizes groups of the faithful to conform themselves ever more closely to the life of the kingdom to come.

Cyprian's solution to the problems of discipline and of schism in which he was involved was one in which the Church's unity and perfection are clearly locked together. The schismatics divided themselves from the Church on grounds of eschatological perfection, whether such perfection was the possession of the schismatics themselves (as with the Novatianists) or of the martyrs exercising eschatological privileges (as with the schism of Felicissimus). Cyprian's theory of the episcopate is one which accommodates itself to the absence of perfection in the body of the faithful and which sees the collegial episcopate as sustainer of the Church's holiness and guarantor of its unity, a unity conceived on constitutional lines.

Augustine both wrote and thought within a social and political context different from that of Tertullian and Cyprian. The ambiguous problems arising out of the great persecution and out of the new position of the Church as the officially sponsored religious body of the empire made imperative a reformulation of the Church's unity and holiness. While holding to episcopate, creed, and sacraments as marks of the one Catholic Church, Augustine discovers the unity of the Church at another level to lie in the Spirit of charity, which will not allow schism to take place even on grounds of holiness. His controversy with the Donatists brought him to a conception of the Church's holiness which distinguishes between the Church as an empirical institution and the Church as the smaller company of those aflame with love of God, who within the empirical Church are on pilgrimage towards a final heavenly destiny. Pelagian perfectionism, together with insistence from monastic quarters upon the crucial necessity of moral freedom, spurred Augustine to a radical doctrine of the elect. His doctrine of election is to be seen in this context as an answer to the question of the Church's holiness within the framework of his doctrine of grace. The whole problem of course is set within the larger context of an imperially sponsored Church whose membership is inclusive of vast numbers who neither by conviction of faith nor by moral fervour would have qualified for the Church of Tertullian's day. Augustine's doctrine of election has here been interpreted as posing a problem respecting the seriousness with which one might, on the basis of this doctrine, take the sacramental life of the empirical Church. *The City of God* then takes up again these various topics, incorporating them into an extended exposition of the theme of the Church as a society and as a culture standing over against the earthly city whose present chief embodiment is the Roman Empire, an empire understood for Augustine's purposes here in largely pagan, pre-Constantinian terms. For Augustine the empirical Church stands as the earthly locus, the external sign, of that inner, heavenly society which moves invisibly in charity and unity towards its transcendent goal.

Leo brings to completion the legal and imperial model of the Church in a theory of papal rule. The Church is a spiritual *imperium* within the temporal *imperium*. The two *imperia* are locked together in mutual inter-relation, a circumstance productive of much tension between their respective rulers. It belongs to the papal ruler to preside over 'binding and loosing', which means that he sets the terms upon which the continuing problem of the moral purity of Church members is repeatedly adjusted to changing requirements.

Gregory introduces a fresh infusion of perfectionist and eschatological thought. Living in the midst of acute duress— social, political, and ecclesiastical—he looks to the coming end and Judgement. Combining monastic spirituality with an Augustinian scheme of elect and reprobate within the Church, he presents us with a view of the Church in which eschatological perfectionism, imminent end, and decisive moral freedom are again brought together. He holds to both the papal theory and the imperial theology which in the thought of Leo had appeared as mutual irritants and which in Gregory appear no less mutually irritating. For Gregory the old imperial theology seems increasingly to lose its relevance so far as the relation of the Byzantine empire to the Church of the West is concerned, though Gregory applies important assumptions from that theology to his relations as pope with the barbarian kingdoms of the West. As occupant of the see of Peter, the centre of the Church's unity, Gregory acts out his sense of responsibility for the Church's eschatological perfection by his zealous efforts to further and protect the monastic life.

The issues which arise for Christians today from this investigation are at least two: the relation of Christian unity to Christian sanctity, and the model upon which Christian unity is conceived.

These pages are written at a time when widespread inertia and indifference appear to be setting in upon the 'ecumenical movement'. The current lull may supply opportunity to reflect upon the traditional relation between 'unity' and 'holiness', i.e. between the structure of the Church as 'one body' and the ethical vocation of the Church as eschatological community. The 'involvement' of the Church in the pressing social and moral issues of our day is the contemporary form of the problem of the Church's holiness. The Church today can be faithful neither to the Gospel itself nor to its own heritage of thought if the problem of the Church's organizational unity is seen as something separable from the contemporary shape of the problem of its sanctity. Organizational structures which serve only to obstruct and to delay the participation of the Church in its present vocation to the world can have very little to commend them. It might be objected here that the very tradition of thought under examination in this book is one which sees the Church as set over against the world and that we see our authors caring intensely for the structure of a specifically Christian society, the Church. That is true enough so far as it goes. It must be recalled, however, that the category, 'world', is ambiguous. Tertullian and Cyprian saw the 'world' as a demonic and idolatrous pagan society, not as a society long under the tutelage of a Christian establishment. Among our authors the time of the Christian establishment is precisely the time in which we see the antithesis of Church and 'world' imported into the Church itself as an antithesis of elect and reprobate, the chief mark of the reprobate being their pride. It is perhaps platitudinous to observe that corporate unconcern over corporate human suffering is not unrelated to pride, and that we have not yet overcome the problem of the demonic 'world' within the Church.

There is no intention here to minimize the urgency of the problem of the Church's unity. The question which must be asked concerns the model upon which such unity is to be conceived, a question which here will find no answer. The New Testament gives to Christians a charge and a promise, but i- does not give them a model valid for every epoch, just as it does not give them a precise pattern of ethical norms valid for all times and places. To suppose that it did would be a failure in historical understanding, which itself would involve them in unfaithfulness to the Gospel. Christians know that the Church in one sense is one and in another sense must be one, but the shape of its unity is a shape to be discovered.

Convinced as they were that the Church is a society parallel to that of the 'world', our authors saw this parallelism as one either of alternatives or of mutual involvement and reciprocal support. In conceiving the Church's unity they naturally chose models from the society which was theirs, the Roman Empire. The imperial model of the Church reaches its most consistent expression in the papal theory of Leo. One has to ask whether and to what degree that theory has any viable religious meaning when the political context within which it was fashioned has long perished. To answer this question would require a disquisition on the meaning and function of religious language, for which (fortunately) there is here no opportunity. I should myself wish to support the view that the papacy, severely revised as to both the theory and the practice of its competence and jurisdiction, ought to serve both as the centre of Christian unity and also as the continuing, eschatological symbol of the political unity of mankind. Inherent in the tradition of thought examined in this book is the assumption that religious unity and political unity, though neither identical nor co-extensive, do in fact imply one another. The one is set off against the other, in one or another of the relations of opposition, uneasy adjustment, or mutual inherence.

My sympathy with both the plight and the vocation of the papacy may be nothing more than a personal prejudice in favour of comprehending unities. In any case, the writers studied here give us more than one model. Tertullian's doctrine of unity in faith summarized by a commonly acknowledged regula is complemented and finally all but superseded by the same author's sectarian church of the Spirit, gathered here and there in groups of two and three. Cyprian's theory of a Church united under a collegial episcopate develops the model drawn from the secular political order but stops short of any conception that would place a governing figure in the Church parallel to the emperor. It might be observed here that to single out, for example, the Cyprianic theory of the episcopate as permanently normative for the Church would seem arbitrary in the extreme. That theory represents one moment in a history of conceptualization of the nature of the Church. By what canons of choice would one detach Cyprian's notion of the unity of the Church under the episcopate from his notion of the Church's holiness, tied as it is so fast and yet so precariously to the episcopate? Or could one possibly suppose that a national church, even one with bishops in apostolic succession, whose 'supreme governor' is a lay secular ruler, is a church that Cyprian would recognize as meeting the minimal requirements of his doctrine? The question may seem polemical, and in part it is. The major point, however, is that Cyprian and every other author studied here must be seen within a historical context that is his and not ours.

Eastern thought about the Church has been left almost wholly out of view in this study: it has been left out in the interest of delineating a tradition of thought possessing both a unity of language and a unity of tendency, and standing in the more immediate background of our problems in the West. The authors studied here have in fact contributed powerfully to the form, language, and content of the problem of the Church as an object of thought in Western Christianity. Though not presenting us with a unified body of teaching, they do present us with what may correctly, if loosely, be called the unity of a tradition. In ringing their changes upon the themes of the unity and holiness of the Church they document two hypotheses: that the problem of the Church tends to be the encompassing problem in Latin patristic thought, and that Latin patristic ecclesiology tends to move between the two poles of the Church's eschatological sanctity and the Church's unity conceived on political and legal models.

It needs to be said immediately that these legal and political conceptions have been complemented by language about the Church as the sphere of the Holy Spirit's activity. It is important to note, however, the varying kinds of relevance which the Spirit has possessed for differing authors according to the varying ways in which unity and holiness have been related to each other. For Tertullian the Spirit is the *Holy* Spirit, enlivening the bands of the saints here and there who have not committed serious sin since their baptism and who constitute the Church by what one might call their unity in moral perfection and striving. For Cyprian the Spirit enlivens the Church of the Catholic episcopate, a thesis which has two important consequences: 1. those who have departed from that Church into schism do not possess the Spirit: 2. bishops committing serious sin cease *ipso facto* to possess any right to act as Catholic bishops and cannot possibly be agents of the Spirit in their sacramental administrations. Augustine's conception of the Church as an inclusive *civitas* brings with it an understanding of the Spirit's role such that the Spirit *of charity* never breaches the Church's unity for reasons of any kind of perfectionism but rather inspires men gladly to endure the presence of 'wheat' and 'tares' within the one empirical Catholic Church. Looking at the matter from Augustine's point of view we would have to say that it is beside the point to charge his doctrine with encouraging laxity in the Church. Rather does it spring from a new level and quality of rigorism. The man who is truly aflame with love of God and who in Augustine's sense loves his Catholic brothers without respect to the level of degradation to which they have fallen is, from a human point of view, not without heroism.

A number of desiderata present themselves today with considerable urgency relative to the work of Church leaders and theologians who, whether or not within official ecumenical dialogue and negotiation, bend their efforts to problems of the nature and form of the Church in our day. It would be nice if one did not have to say 'Church leaders *and* theologians'. But the seclusion of theologians in institutions of higher learning and solemn assurances from bishops and leading clergy that they are *not* theologians are unfortunate facts of our present duress. It is earnestly to be desired that men and women concerned with these problems should be thoroughly aware of materials of the sort that have been studied in this book. Work in and for the Church that is not undertaken with an informed sense of responsibility to the Christian past is not *theological* work, however good its intentions may be.

But on the other hand it is also much to be hoped that those who by disposition are inclined towards respect for the past will come to be fully apprised of the degree to which the great fathers of the Church were in their own times innovators. To think and to act in the spirit of Cyprian and of Augustine would certainly not be to cling to the precise doctrines which they formulated and to the policies which they defended, and to cling to these for no other reason than that they are doctrines and policies of Cyprian and of Augustine. To do such would not be to follow the example of Cyprian relative to Tertullian nor of Augustine relative to Cyprian. In his book, *Contours of Faith*, John Dillenberger has cogently argued that the repetition of a precise theological formulation from one cultural context to another has resulted even in a complete reversal of meaning from that of the original formula. Certainly the cultural shifts occurring in the period stretching from the end of the second century to the beginning of the seventh were less marked than the cultural distance which separates us from that entire period; yet precisely in the earlier period do we find occurring the marked changes of thought which the preceding chapters have pointed out. Careful study and comparison of what the great fathers wrote and did leads to the conclusion that on the whole they knew implicitly that new occasions teach new duties and that time makes ancient good uncouth. The astonishing thing about the fathers is the resolution with which they introduce and rationalize novelty in spite of what we would call their frequently unhistorical assumptions concerning the unchanging character of Christian truth.

Finally, the hope cannot be suppressed that those charged with finding practical and institutional solutions to current problems will carry out their work with no less *theological* zeal than that which characterized the authors studied here. True it is that our five authors are not equal in stature to each other as theologians. Yet each reacted instinctively to the issues which he faced in such a way as to press at least the elements of a theology from the manifold harvest presented to him by scripture, Church tradition, historical situation, and the linguistic and conceptual tools supplied by his culture. Theology is an activity essential to the well-being of the Christian Church, though it does at times go into eclipse.

NOTES

CHAPTER 1

1 *Scap.*, 3
2 *Acta Scillit.*
3 Cf. *Apol.*, 33
4 *Nat.*, II.1
5 Mark 13.9; John 15.20; 2 Thess. 5.3; Heb. 13.14; Phil. 3.20; Rev. 2.12f; 17.1–18.24
6 *Fug.*, 10; *Idol.*, 19; *Cor. Mil.*, 11; *Pud.*, 16 & 21
7 *Bapt.*, 15
8 *Orat.*, 2
9 Gal. 4.26; Rev. 21.2; *Marc.*, III.25
10 *An.*, 43
11 *Exhort. Cast.*, 5; *Mon.*, 3 & 14
12 *Cult. Fem.*, II.7 & 9
13 *Apol.*, 38
14 Ibid., 21
15 *Idol.*, 17
16 Ibid., 1
17 Ibid., 10 & 11
18 Ibid., 11
19 Ibid., 19; *Cor. Mil.*, 11
20 *Ux.*, II.3
21 *Idol.*, 23
22 *Spect.*, *passim*
23 Ibid., 15
24 Ibid., 1
25 *Idol.*, 7
26 Luke 14.28–30; *Idol.*, 12
27 Ibid., 24
28 Ibid.; *Cor. Mil.*, 13
29 *Idol.*, 8 & 11
30 Ibid., 16
31 Ibid., 10
32 Ibid.

33 *Nat.*, 1.18
34 *Pat.*, 2 & 3
35 Ibid., 5 & 11
36 *Scorp.*, *passim*; *Fug.*; cf. *Ux.*, 1.3; *Pat.*, 13
37 *Mart.*, 1 & 2; *Scorp.*, 9
38 Ibid., 6
39 *Mart.*, 1
40 *Exhort. Cast.*, 7; *Orat.*, 19; Bapt., 17
41 *Cor. Mil.*, 13
42 *Orat.*, 19; *Apol*, 16; *Idol.*, 19; *Mart.*, 3; *Cor. Mil.*, 1
43 *Cor. Mil.*, 13; *Spect.*, 30
44 *Apol.*, 17; cf. *Test. An.*, *passim*
45 *Apol.*, 30–5
46 Ibid., 5; *Jud.*, 2
47 *Apol.*, 30, 32f, 39
48 *Nat.*, 1.7; *Apol.*, 39
49 *Apol.*, 21; *Prax.*, 7, 11 & 21
50 *Praescr. Haer.*, 13 & 20
51 Ibid., 13 & 37; *Marc.*, 1.21; IV.5
52 *Praescr. Haer.*, 15, 20f, 28, 32, 36f
53 *Mon.*, 2
54 *Virg. Vel.*, 2
55 Ibid., 1
56 Ibid.; cf. *Cor. Mil.*, 4
57 *Ux.*, II.8; *Idol.*, 2; *Virg. Vel.*, 2
58 *Pud.*, 11
59 *Virg. Vel.* 1, 2 & 3
60 *Praescr. Haer.*, 26 & 30; cf. *Marc.*, II.17; III.21 & 22
61 *Praescr. Haer.*, 28; cf. 13
62 *Virg. Vel.*, 1
63 *Mon.*, 3. See the whole treatise and also the whole of *Virg. Vel.*
64 *Prax.*, 2, 8 & 30
65 *Pat.*, 5; *Apol.*, 39, 44 & 46
66 *Paen.*, 9
67 Ibid., 10
68 Ibid., 5 & 7
69 Ibid., 6; *Bapt.*, 18
70 *Pud.*, 1 & 19
71 Ibid., 1 (fin.)
72 Ibid., 21; Matt. 16.18f
73 *Pud.*, 21; *Exhort. Cast.*, 4
74 *Pud.*, 21
75 *An.*, 11

76 *Pud.*, 21
77 Ibid.
78 Ibid., 22

CHAPTER 2

1 *Demet.*, 4 & 5
2 Ibid., 12 & 13
3 *Exhortat. Mart.*, 11
4 Ibid., *Praef.*, 4
5 Ibid.
6 Tertullian, *Apol.*, 4
7 Tertullian, *Paen.*, 5–7
8 Tertullian, *Jej.*, 3
9 *Op. et Eleemos.*, 5
10 Ibid., 18
11 Ibid., 14 & 15
12 Ibid., 21
13 Tertullian, *Ux.*, 1.3; *Pat.*, 13
14 Matt. 10.23
15 *Epp.* 7; 14.1; 59.6
16 *Laps.*, 7
17 Ibid., 27; *Epp.* 30.3; 55.13
18 *Ep.*, 43.1
19 *Testim.*, III.28; *Laps.*, 17 & 20
20 *Ep.*, 55.27
21 *Laps.*, 17–20
22 Ibid., 18 & 20
23 Ibid., 17
24 *Epp.* 30.8; 55.5
25 *Epp.* 18.1; 20.3
26 *Ep.* 55.3 & 7.
27 *Ep.* 25
28 *Ep.* 55.6, 17 & 20
29 *Ep.* 56
30 *Ep.* 57.3 & 4
31 *Ep.* 59.16
32 *Epp.* 55.21; 57.5; 68.5; 69.10 & 17
33 *de Dominica Oratione*, 23; *Unit.*, 6 & 14
34 *Ep.* 33.1
35 *Ep.* 59.5
36 *Ep.* 57.5
37 *Ep.* 3.3
38 *Ep.* 55.20 & 21

39 *Epp.* 66.4; 75.16
40 *Ep.* 68.4
41 *Unit.*, 4
42 *Ep.* 43.5
43 *Epp.* 68.1 & 3; 55.24 & 30
44 *Unit.*, 5
45 *Epp.* 45.1; 55.7 and 30; 68.1; *Mort.*, 19
46 *Ep.* 55.24
47 *Ep.* 66.8
48 *Ep.* 55.8 & 24
49 *Ep.* 27.3
50 *Unit.*, 6
51 *Ep.* 73.21; *Unit.*, 14
52 *Unit.*, 23; *Ep.* 75.3
53 Tertullian, *Prax.*, 3
54 *Unit.*, 5
55 Ibid., 5; *Epp.* 45.1; 48.3
56 See, e.g. *Epp.* 49.2; 66.8; cf. *Unit.*, 5; *Ep.*, 55.24
57 *Epp.* 54.3; 55.15 & 25
58 *Epp.* 54.3; 55.25; 59.16
59 *Ep.* 55.29
60 *Ep.* 55.27 & 28
61 *Ep.* 56.1.
62 *Ep.* 55.14 & 26
63 *Laps.*, 17; *Ep.* 54.3; John 13.16
64 *Ep.* 33.1
65 *Ep.* 63.14
66 *Ep.* 67.2
67 *Ep.* 67.1; Lev. 21.17
68 *Epp.* 55.11; 67.1, 6, 8
69 *Ep.* 68.2
70 *Epp.* 58.1 & 7; 59.13; 67.7; *Unit.*, 10 & 16
71 *Epp.* 67.3 & 6; 68.2 & 3; 69.9
72 *Ep.* 67.3
73 *Epp.* 73.4; 74.1 & 5
74 *Epp.* 73.5; 74.1
75 *Ep.* 74.1
76 *Epp.* 69.11; 72.1; 74.5; 73.4 & 6
77 See, *e.g.*, Tertullian, *Bapt.*, 6–8
78 *Epp.* 74.5; 75.8
79 *Ep.* 75.18
80 *Epp.* 71.3; 75.17
81 *Epp.* 74.8; 75.6 & 24f

82 *Ep.* 75.25
83 *Epp.* 69.8 & 11; 70.1; 73.1; 74.4 & 5
84 *Ep.* 69.11
85 *Ep.* 74.5
86 *Epp.* 70.3; 72.1
87 *Epp.* 71.3; 73.13
88 *Ep.* 68.5
89 *Ep.* 67.2–4 & 8f.; 65.3f
90 *Ep.* 55.21
91 *Epp.* 73.26; 69.17

CHAPTER 3

1 *Acta Saturnini*, 21
2 Augustine, *c. Litt. Patil.*, II.85
3 *Ep.* 185.12; Theodoret, *Haeret. Fab. Comp.*, IV.6
4 *Brevic. Collat. cum Donat.*, III.25
5 *c. Crescon.*, III.30
6 *c. Ep. Parmeniani*, II.8 & 12f.; *c, Litt. Petil.*, II.90 & 117; *c. Crescon.*, I.33; II.27; VI.53
7 *c. Crescon.*, II.27
8 *Ep.* 93.43
9 Cyprian, *Epp.* 67.1–3, 9; 70.1; 73.6
10 Cyprian, *Epp.* 69.17; 73.26
11 *c. Ep. Parmeniani*, III.29; *c. Crescon.*, III.22; IV.5, 16, 22, 42; *Gesta cum Emerito*, 10
12 *de Bapt.*, II.14; III.2f
13 Optatus, *de Schism. adv. Parmenian.*, II.2; Augustine, *de Bapt.*, II.2; *Ep.* 43.7
14 *de Bapt.*, II.9
15 *c. Crescon.*, II.4
16 *de Bapt.*, 1.2, 9 & 10
17 *c. Crescon.*, II.15
18 *c. Litt. Petil.*, I.2
19 *Epp.* 23.2, 6; 44.8; 106.1
20 *de Bapt.*, I.1
21 Ibid., 1.27f
22 Ibid., II.7
23 Ibid., II.7f; III.3
24 Ibid., IV.18
25 Ibid., IV.12; Cyprian, *Laps.*, 6
26 Ibid., 10 & 34
27 Ibid., 34
28 *Ep.* 43.25; cf. *c. Ep. Parmeniani*, II.4
29 Ps. 72.11

30 *c. Litt. Petil.*, II.202–7; *c. Crescon.*, III.56; *Epp.* 87.8; 93.9–19

31 *de Bapt.*, IV.18; *c. Litt. Petil.*, III.3 & 43; Matt. 13.24–30, 36–40, 47f; 25.31–46

32 *c. Litt. Petil.*, III.3 & 43

33 *Unit.*, 7. See also, e.g. *c. Litt. Petil*, II.247; *Enarr. in Ps.*, 63.2; 148.8; *Ep.* 261.2; *Tract. in Joann. Evang.*, 28.1; *de civ. Dei*, 21.15

34 *Retract.*, II.44; cf. *de Bapt.*, V.21

35 *Epp.* 43.22; 44.11; *de Pat.*, 8; cf. 10 & 24f

36 *c. Ep. Parmeniani*, II.39 & 42; III.2

37 *Ep.* 53.3

38 *c. Ep. Parmeniani*, II.12; *c. Litt. Petil.*, I.8

39 *Ep.* 93.36

40 *c. Crescon.*, III.39

41 *c. Litt. Petil.*, II.172; *Ep.* 185.48–50

42 *c. Ep. Parmeniani*, III.28; *Ep.* 93.23

43 Ibid.; *c. Litt. Petil*, II.90

44 Optatus, *de Schism. adv. Parmenian.*, III.2

45 *Epp.* 43.7; 53.2; 209; *de Bapt.* II.2; *c. Crescon.*, II.46; *c. Julian.*, I.13; *c. duas Epp. Pelag.*, I.2

46 *de Bapt.*, IV.29; III.19; *Epp.* 89.7; 93.46

47 *de Bapt.*, II.12f; IV.24; *Epp.* 88.9; 93.46; 108.4 & 6

48 *de Bapt.*, III.21

49 Ibid., IV.5; VII.100

50 Ibid., IV.5

51 Ibid., III.23; VII.99f

CHAPTER 4

1 See, e.g. Tertullian, *Exhort. Cast.*, 2; Justin Martyr, *Apol.*, i, 43f

2 *Pelagius's Expositions of Thirteen Epistles of St Paul*, ed. A. Souter (Cambridge 1926), 128, 12; 484, 3; 512, 12; *Ep. ad Demetriad.*, 24; *de Lege*, 1; *Virg.*, 11

3 *Exp.*, 378, 5 (MS v)

4 Ibid., 356, 12ff

5 *de Lege*, 1

6 See, e.g. *Exp.* 72.13–21; 197, 14; 346, 3; 358, 6ff

7 Tertullian, *Paen.*, 9

8 For Pelagius see, e.g. *Exp.*, 353, 1ff

9 For Tertullian, see, e.g. *Exhort. Cast.*, 2

10 Pelagius, *Exp.*, 474, 2

11 Augustine, *de Nat. et Grat.*, 14

12 Pelagius, *Exp.*, 151, 20ff; 327, 15; *Virg.* 8

13 *de Lege*, 4f; *Ep. ad Demetriad.*, 16; *Cel.*, 5f

14 *de Lege*, 5; *Cel.*, 5f

15 See in Augustine, *de Nat. et Grat.*, 21

M

16 Augustine, *de Spir. et Lit.*, 1 & 3

17 *de Dono Persev.*, 4 & 8

18 *ad Simplic. de Div. Quaest.*, 1.2.21

19 de *Civ. Dei.*, XXII.30

20 *de Corrept. et Grat.*, 18f.

21 *de Dono Persev.*, 21

22 Ibid.

23 *de Bapt.*, 5.38

24 *de Corrept. et Grat.*, 42; cf. *de Dono Persev.*, 19

25 Ibid., 31; *de Nat. et Grat.*, 35 & 62; *de Grat. et Lib. Arbit*, 27 & 33–8

26 *de Corrept. et Grat.*, 12; *de Praedest, Sanct.*, 23

27 *de Corrept. et Grat.*, 31

28 E.g. *de Bapt.*, 5.38

29 *de Spir. et Lit.*, 60; *de Grat. et Lib. Arbit.*, 44; *de Corrept. et Grat.*, 18f, etc.

30 Rom. 11.33 (RSV)

31 E.g. *de An. et ejus Orig.*, 1.11; 11.14; *c. duas Epp. Pelag.*, 11.8; *de Corrept. et Grat.*, 18

32 *de Dono Persev.*, 18f; cf. ibid., 31ff; *de Spir. et Lit.*, 60

33 *de Dono Persev.*, 25 & 16; cf. *de Gestis Pelag.*, 34f

34 *de Praedest. Sanct.*, 35f

35 *de Pecc. Mer., et de Bapt. Inf.* 1.23–8

36 Ibid., 29f

37 *de Grat. et Lib. Arbit.*, 44f; *de Praedest. Sanct.*, 23; *de Dono Persev.*, 25

38 *de Pecc. Mer.*, 1. 30; *de Grat. et Lib. Arbit.*, 45

39 *de Corrept. et Grat.*, 12

40 *de Grat. et Lib. Arbit.*, 45

41 *Retract.*, 2.69

42 E.g. *de Civ. Dei*, III.17

43 Ibid., 1.7

44 Ibid., XXII.11f., & 25–8

45 Ibid., 11.3

46 Ibid., XVIII.52

47 Ibid., v.26, cf. v.21; v.23

48 Ibid., 1. praef.; 1.30f.; XIV.28; XIX.26

49 Ibid., v.26

50 Ibid.

51 Ibid., XVIII.51; cf. 11.19; XVIII.49; XX.8, etc.

52 See, e.g. *Ep.* 238

53 *Ep.* 220.7

54 *de Gen. ad Lit.*, v.9

55 *c. Academicos*, 11 .22

56 *de Civ. Dei*, XI.23

57 Ibid., x.25

58 *de Bapt.*, II.6; cf. Lk. 20.36
59 *de Civ. Dei.*, X.7
60 Ibid., XXII.1
61 Ibid., XI.9
62 Ibid., XI.13
63 Ibid., XI.13 & 28
64 Ibid., XI.13; XII.9
65 Ibid., XII.9; Rom. 5.5
66 Ibid., XII.9
67 Ibid., XI.18
68 *de Dono Persev.*, 41
69 *de Civ. Dei*, XX.9
70 Ibid., XX.8
71 Ibid., I.35
72 *On True Religion*, 50
73 *de Civ. Dei*, XI.1; Ps. 87.3
74 *de Civ. Dei*, XIX.21
75 Ibid., XIX.21 & 24
76 Ibid., XIV.28; XIX.24
77 Ibid., XII.1; XXI.1; *de Gen. ad Lit.*, XI.20
78 *de Civ. Dei*, I.30f; III.21; XIX.7
79 Ibid., XVIII.22
80 Ibid., V.15
81 Ibid., IV.15
82 Ibid., I. *praef*; XI.1; XVII.4 & 16
83 Ibid., XIV.28
84 Ibid., V.18
85 Ibid., IX.4f
86 Ibid., IX.15
87 Ibid., X.6 & 20
88 Ibid., XI.1
89 Ibid., XX.26
90 Ibid., XVIII.54
91 *Enarr. in Ps.*, 62.8
92 *de Civ. Dei.*, XIX.6; cf. V.19
93 Ibid., V.24f
94 Ibid., XIX.17 & 26
95 Ibid., XIX.17
96 *Epp.* 133f & 153.3
97 *Ep.* 220.3
98 *de Civ. Dei*, XVII.6; XIX.17, 19
99 Ibid., XVIII.51
100 Ibid., XV.1

101 Ibid., xv.2; xvi.3; xvii.3–14; xviii.41; *Enarr. in Ps.*, 148.16
102 *de Civ. Dei*, xvi.12; cf. ibid., 12–34; xviii.27
103 Ibid., xviii.8
104 Ibid., xviii.46
105 Ibid., x.5; xviii.48
106 Ibid., xx.5 & 9

CHAPTER 5

 1 Leo, *Ep.* 82.1
 2 *Ep.* 44.3
 3 *Ep.* 45.3
 4 *Epp.* 24.1; 69.2
 5 *Ep.* 162.1
 6 *Ep.* 135.1
 7 *Ep.* 169.1
 8 *Ep.* 113.1
 9 *Ep.* 156.6
10 *Ep.* 78
11 *Epp.* 29; 30.1; 84.1; 117.2
12 *Epp.* 24.1; 156.3 & 6
13 *Epp.* 23.1; 24.1; 126; 141.2
14 *Epp.* 89; 93.1
15 *Ep.* 156.3
16 *Ep.* 162.2f; cf. 144; 146.1; 156.1–3
17 See *Epp.* 43.4; 44.3; cf. 114.1
18 *Epp.* 43.3; 44.3
19 *Epp.* 33.2; 93.1
20 *Ep.* 28
21 *Epp.* 33.2; 82; 90.2
22 *Ep.* 98.1
23 *Ep.* 104.3
24 *Ep.* 5.2
25 *Serm.* 3.3
26 *Serm.*, 5.5
27 *Ep.* 119.2; cf. *Serm.*, 16.6
28 *Ep.* 10.1
29 *Serm.*, 83.1
30 *Ep.* 9. *praef.*
31 *Ep.* 14.11; cf. Cyprian, *Unit.*, 4
32 *Serm.*, 4.2f
33 *Serm.*, 3.3
34 *Serm.*, 3.3f
35 *Ep.* 45.2

36 *Serm.*, 5.4
37 Cf. *Serm.*, 1.2; 82.1–4
38 *Ep.* 104.3
39 *Ep.* 104.3
40 *Ep.* 11
41 *Serm.*, 82.1
42 Gregory, *Epp.* II.48; III.30; VII.40; IX.59, 109, 117. 122, etc.
43 *Epp.* I.25; III.10; IV.3 & 39; VI.2; VII.4
44 *Ep.* VII.40
45 *Epp.* IX.59 & 108; XI.47, 55–7
46 *Ep.* V.20
47 *Epp.* I.1; I.25; XI.45
48 *Moralia in Job*, XXXII.35
49 *Ep.* XIV.17; *Regula* I.3; II.6
50 *Epp.* I.36; II.11, 31, 47; IX.4; X.62; V.20; *Mor.*, XIX.23; XX.79; XXII.53; *Regula*, III.
51 *Epp.* IV.6; XIV.4; XIII.18; X.67
52 *Epp.* I.72; XIII.18; XIV.4
53 *Ep.* II.31
54 *Ep.* V.20
55 *Ep.* III.65
56 *Mor.*, XXXI.4
57 *Ep.* XI.47
58 Ibid.
59 *Ep.* III.65
60 *Epp.* IX.11, 109f, 122; XI.59f, 63
61 *Mor.*, *Praef.* 14 & 16; VII.29
62 Ibid., praef. 15
63 Ibid., 14
64 Ibid., 19
65 Cf. *Ep.* X.37, etc.
66 *Mor.*, XIV.27; XV.32f, 69; XVI.15; XXXII.25–28; XXXIII.63; XXXIV.8
67 *Epp.* V.18 and 21
68 *Epp.* I.36; II.32
69 *Ep.* IX.65
70 *Ep.* III.56
71 *Mor.* VIII.50; IX.50; XII.19 and 59f; XVI.33; XXII.50; XXX.53; XXXI.101; XXXV.42. *Ep.* III.65
72 *Ep.* III.59
73 E.g. *Ep.* IV.18
74 *Mor.*, XVIII.68
75 Ibid., XIX.43ff
76 Ibid., XVI.57
77 Ibid., VI.57; XIX.43f; XXIV.23

78 Ibid., II.75, cf. I.40; IV.58ff; xxx.8
79 *Epp.* I.5f
80 *Ep.* IX.121
81 *Ep.* v.39
82 *Mor.* v.5; XVIII.70
83 Ibid., XVI.30; XVIII.63; XXXIII.38ff
84 Ibid., xxv.20
85 Ibid., IV.42ff; IX.90ff; XXXI.12
86 Ibid., XI.52
87 Ibid., VII.29f
88 Ibid., IX.90ff
89 Ibid., XIII.9 & 27
90 Ibid., XIX. 16ff; xx. 52
91 Ibid., XII.33; XVIII.27; cf. XIX.15 & 27; xx.16
92 Ibid., III.35; VI.1; VII.30; VIII.66ff; xx.77
93 Ibid., xxv.21
94 Ibid., xx.51; XXXI.28
95 Ibid., VI.41
96 Ibid., XXI.36
97 Ibid., XVIII.48

BIBLIOGRAPHY

GENERAL WORKS

General surveys of patristic thought about the Church are not numerous. Probably the most useful, though it goes only to the fourth century, is G. Bardy, *La théologie de l'Eglise* (Paris 1947). Tertullian, Cyprian, and Augustine are treated in E. Altendorf, *Einheit und Heiligkeit der Kirche* (Berlin and Leipzig 1932). For the problem of schism generally in the patristic period see S. L. Greenslade, *Schism in the Early Church* (London 1963; New York n.d.). Treatments of particular topics, also in the earlier period, are to be found in H. B. Swete, ed., *Essays on the Early History of the Church and Ministry* (2nd edn., London 1921). On various aspects of the development of the episcopate, see Wm Telfer, *The Office of a Bishop* (London 1962), and H. U. Instinsky, *Bischofstuhl und Kaiserthron* (Munich 1955). For the general topic of the relation of Church and State, see especially T. M. Parker, *Christianity and the State in the Light of History* (London 1955). On the relation between the early church and pagan society, see C. J. Cadoux, *The Early Church and the World* (Edinburgh 1925) and J. A. Crook, *Law and Life of Rome* (London 1967). A magisterial work on the social, economic, and administrative history of the Roman Empire is provided by A. H. M. Jones, *The Later Roman Empire*, 3 vols. and maps (Oxford 1964). Useful surveys of Roman law are those of W. W. Buckland, *A Text-Book of Roman Law from Augustus to Justinian* (Cambridge 1963, third edition revised by Peter Stein) and H. F. Jolowicz, *Historical Introduction to the Study of Roman Law* (Cambridge, 1952). A useful tool for discovering the meaning and usage of words in Roman legal texts is the Heumann-Seckel *Handlexikon zu den Quellen des römischen Rechts* (10th edn. Graz 1958). A fine survey of the development of penitential practice is that of Wm Telfer, *The Forgiveness of Sins* (London 1959; Philadelphia 1960); K. E. Kirk, *The Vision of God* (2nd edn. London 1932) is also important. For thought and practice concerning martyrdom consult, though with caution, W. H. C. Frend, *Martyrdom and Persecution in the Early Church* (Oxford

1965). For shrewd comments on the relation between pagan political thought and Christian theology the present book is indebted to Arnold A. T. Ehrhardt, *Politische Metaphysik von Solon bis Augustin*, 3 vols. (Tübingen 1959–69). Short, general sketches of Tertullian, Cyprian, and Augustine are easily available in Hans von Campenhausen, *Lateinische Kirchenväter* (Stuttgart 1964), E. T., *The Latin Fathers* (London 1964), published in U.S.A. as *Men Who Shaped the Western Church* (New York 1964).

I

TERTULLIAN:
THE UNITY OF THE SPIRIT AND THE ONE FAITH

English translations of works of Tertullian are to be found in vols. 3 and 4 of *The Ante-Nicene Fathers* (Grand Rapids, Mich. n.d.) and in *The Ante-Nicene Christian Library* (Edinburgh 1870). Less extensive selections from his writings are available in vol. 5 of *The Library of Christian Classics* and in the series from the Newman Press, *Ancient Christian Writers*.

Introductory studies of Tertullian's theology may be found in A. d'Alès, *La théologie de Tertullien* (Paris 1905) and T. D. Barnes, *Tertullian: a Historical and Literary Study* (Oxford 1971). The delicate relations between Tertullian's language and his theology are explored in R. Braun, *Deus Christianorum: recherches sur le vocabulaire doctrinal de Tertullien* (Paris 1962). On Montanism see the article under that title by G. Salmon in the *Dictionary of Christian Biography*.

Of relevance to particular problems explored in the present chapter are the following: Karl Adam, *Der Kirchenbegriff Tertullians* (Paderborn 1907); A. Beck, *Römisches Recht bei Tertullian und Cyprian* (Halle 1930); A. A. T. Ehrhardt, 'Das Corpus Christi und die Korporation im spät-römischen Recht', in *Zeitschrift der Savigny-stiftung für Rechtsgeschichte*, Röm. Abt 70 (1953) and 71 (1954); F. C. Grant, 'Religio Licita', in *Texte und Untersuchungen*, vol. 79; Hugo Koch, *Kallist und Tertullian* (Heidelberg 1920); George La Piana, 'The Roman Church at the End of the Second Century', in *Harvard Theological Review*, 18 (1925); Jaroslav Pelikan, 'The Eschatology of Tertullian', in *Church History* 21 (1952); V. Morel, 'Le développement de la "discipline" sous l'action de Saint Esprit chez Tertullien', in *Revue d'Histoire Ecclésiastique* 35 (1939); Wm Telfer, 'The Origins of Christianity in Africa', in *Texte und Untersuchungen*, vol. 79; J. P. Waltzing, 'Collegia', in *Dictionnaire d'Archéologie chrétienne et de liturgie*, vol. 3, cols. 2107–40; A. P. Maistre, '*Traditio*—Aspects théologiques d'un terme de droit chez Tertullien', in *Revue des Sciences Philosophiques et Théologiques*, 51 (1967).

2

CYPRIAN: THE EPISCOPAL BOND OF PEACE

An English translation of the works of Cyprian is to be found in vol. 5 of *The Ante-Nicene Fathers*. It is to be noted, however, that the numbering of Cyprian's letters in that volume does not correspond to the numbering used in the present chapter, which is that employed in the edition of G. Hartel, *Corpus Scriptorum Ecclesiasticorum Latinorum*, vol. III, part ii; the editor of the English translation provides in an annotation the number of each letter according to the system used here. An English translation of the letters employing the system of numbers used here may be found in vol. 51 of the series, *The Fathers of the Church*. For the two treatises, *de Unitate* and *de Lapsis*, the translation and notes of Maurice Bévenot in vol. 25 of *Ancient Christian Writers* should be consulted.

The classic general study of Cyprian in English is still E. W. Benson, *Cyprian* (London 1897). A survey of Cyprian's theology is available in A. d'Alès, *La théologie de St Cyprien* (Paris 1922). A more recent study is that of G. S. M. Walker, *The Churchmanship of St Cyprian* (London 1968). The solution assumed in the present chapter to the difficult question of the literary relation between the two recensions of the work *de Unitate* is that argued by M. Bévenot, *St Cyprian's 'De Unitate' chapter 4 in the Light of the Manuscripts* (Rome Analecta Gregoriana, 1938); for important support of this view the reader should also consult O. Perler, 'Zur Datierung der beiden Fassungen des vierten Kapitels De Unitate Ecclesiae', in *Römische Quartalschrift* 44 (1936). See also M. Bévenot, *The Tradition of the Manuscripts: Studies in the Transmission of St Cyprian's Treatises* [including text of *de Unitate*] (Oxford 1961).

Further studies on particular matters under consideration here are as follows: J. H. Bernard, 'The Cyprianic Doctrine of the Ministry', in H. B. Swete, ed., *Essays on the Early History of the Church and Ministry* (2nd edn, London 1921); A. Beck, *Römisches Recht*, noted above under ch. 1; Hugo Koch, *Cathedra Petri* (Giessen 1930), and *Cyprianische Untersuchungen* (Bonn 1926); G. W. H. Lampe, *The Seal of the Spirit: a Study in the Doctrine of Baptism and Confirmation in the New Testament and the Fathers* (London 1951); M. A. Fahey, *Cyprian and the Bible: a Study in Third-Century Exegesis* (Tübingen 1971). M. Réveillaud, 'Note pour une pneumatologie Cyprienne', in *Texte und Untersuchungen* 81; M. Simon, 'Le Judaisme berbère dans l'Afrique ancienne', in *Revue d'Histoire et de Philosophie Religieuses* 26 (1946), pp. 1–31 and 105–45; M. F. Wiles, 'The Theological Legacy of St Cyprian', in *Journal of Ecclesiastical History* 14 (1963).

3

THE DONATISTS AND AUGUSTINE:
FORBEARING ONE ANOTHER IN LOVE

An English translation by J. R. King of three of Augustine's Anti-Donatist works is available in vol. 3 of *The Works of Aurelius Augustine*, ed. Marcus Dods (Edinburgh 1872).

The most comprehensive survey of Donatism is that provided by W. H. C. Frend, *The Donatist Church* (Oxford 1952). For an important corrective to Frend's sociological and economic interpretation of the movement, see Emin Tengström, *Donatisten und Katholiken* (Götenborg, Sweden, 1964). On both the Donatists and Augustine consult Jean-Paul Brisson, *Autonomisme et Christianisme dans l'Afrique romaine* (Paris 1958) and G. G. Willis, *Saint Augustine and the Donatist Controversy* (London 1950). B. Lohse, 'Kaiser und Papst im Donatistenstreit', in G. Kretschmar and B. Lohse, edd., *Ecclesia und Res Publica* (Göttingen 1961).

Biographical treatments of Augustine are provided by Peter Brown, *Augustine of Hippo* (London; Los Angeles 1967) and Gerald Bonner, *St Augustine of Hippo* (London; Philadelphia 1963). A most important study of the religion of Augustine is that of John Burnaby, *Amor Dei* (London 1938). Augustine's doctrine of the Church is treated in Thomas Specht, *Die Lehre von der Kirche nach dem heiligen Augustine* (Paderborn 1892). Augustine's philosophy and his relation to Platonism are discussed by R. A. Markus in *The Cambridge History of Later Greek and Early Medieval Philosophy*, ed. A. H. Armstrong (Cambridge 1967), pp. 341–419. On the same topic, see also A. H. Armstrong, *St Augustine and Christian Platonism* (Villanova, Pa., 1967), and John F. Callahan, *Augustine and the Greek Philosophers* (Villanova, Pa., 1967).

4

AUGUSTINE:
THE CHURCH OF THE ELECT AND THE TWO CITIES

English translations of most of Augustine's anti-Pelagian treatises may be found in vol. 5, first series, of *A Select Library of Nicene and Post-Nicene Fathers* (Grand Rapids, Mich., 1956). A translation by Marcus Dods of the complete *City of God* is available in a volume of *The Modern Library*, published by Random House, New York; a more recent and superior translation by a number of scholars is available in seven volumes of the Loeb Classical Library.

On the issues treated in this chapter, the reader may be referred to the relevant chapters in the biographies noted above by Bonner and Brown. There is a general study of Pelagius by John Ferguson (*Pelagius: a historical and theological study*, Cambridge, Eng. 1956). For a discussion of particular problems related to Pelagius and the controversy, see Robert F. Evans, *Pelagius: Inquiries and Reappraisals* (London; New York 1968); for the literary problem of identifying Pelagius' extant writings, consult the same author's *Four Letters of Pelagius* (London; New York 1968). See also Torgny Bohlin, *Die Theologie des Pelagius und ihre Genesis* (Uppsala 1957). On the predestinarian question see the important work of Gotthard Nygren, *Das Prädestinationsproblem in der Theologie Augustins* (Lund 1956).

Books and articles on *The City of God* and problems related thereto are legion. Among the more useful may be cited the following: Christopher Dawson, 'St Augustine and his Age', in M. C. D'Arcy *et al*, *Saint Augustine* (Meridian paperback, Cleveland and New York, 1964, sixth printing); Edward R. Hardy, 'The City of God', in Roy W. Battenhouse, ed., *A Companion to the Study of St Augustine* (New York 1955); John J. O'Meara, *Charter of Christendom: The Significance of The City of God* (New York 1961); A Lauras and H. Rondet, 'Le thème des deux cités dans l'œuvre de saint Augustin' (*Études Augustiniennes*, Paris 1953); E. Lamirande, *L'Église céleste selon saint Augustin* (*Études Augustiniennes*, Paris 1963); B. Lohse, 'Zu Augustins Engellehre', in *Zeitschrift für Kirchengeschichte* 70 (1959) and 'Augustins Wandlung in seiner Beurteilung des Staates', in *Texte und Untersuchungen* 81; Lloyd G. Patterson, *God and History in Early Christian Thought* (London; New York 1967); R. A. Markus, *Saeculum: history and Society in the Theology of Saint Augustine* (Cambridge 1970).

5

LEO AND GREGORY:
THE PAPAL PRINCIPATE AND THE CHURCH IN AFFLICTION

Selected sermons and letters of Leo, and selected letters of Gregory, are available in English translation in vols. 12 and 13, second series, of *A Select Library of Nicene and Post-Nicene Fathers*. It is to be noted that the system of numbering of Gregory's letters employed in the present chapter is that found in this English translation, which is also that in the Migne *Patrologia Latina*. The best Latin text of Gregory's letters is that of P. Ewald and L. Hartmann (*Monumenta Germaniae Historica*, 1899), whose numbering is different; on pp. xxxviii–xliii in vol. 2 of their edition they supply a comparative table of the two systems of numbering. An English translation of Gregory's *Moralia* is to be found in the series, *A Library of Fathers of the Holy Catholic Church* (Oxford 1844–50).

Among books on the papacy the following may be mentioned: T. G. Jalland, *The Church and the Papacy* (London; New York 1944); Karl F. Morrison, *Tradition and Authority in the Western Church* (Princeton 1969); Walter Ullmann, *The Growth of Papal Government in the Middle Ages* (2nd edn, London 1962).

The standard biography in English of Leo is that of T. G. Jalland, *The Life and Times of St Leo the Great* (London; New York 1941). The present chapter is especially indebted to the following: H. M. Klinkenberg, 'Papsttum und Reichskirche bei Leo d. Gr.', in *Zeitschrift der Savigny-Stiftung für Rechtsgeschichte*, Kan. Abt. 38 (1952); Peter Stockmeier, *Leo I des Grossen Beurteilung der kaiserlichen Religionspolitik* (Munich 1959); Walter Ullmann, 'Leo I and the Theme of Papal Primacy', in *Journal of Theological Studies*, n.s., XI.i (1960).

The classic English biography of Gregory is that of F. Homes Dudden, *Gregory the Great*, 2 vols. (London, 1905); a one-volume life is that by P. Batiffol, *Saint Gregory the Great* (E.T., New York 1929). Of particular importance for the present chapter has been Remigius Rudmann, *Mönchtum und kirchlicher Dienst in den Schriften Gregors des Grossen* (Sankt-Ottilien 1956).

INDEX